Orchids

Barkeria cyclotella (see page 72)

Orchids

Revised Edition

Joyce Stewart

TIMBER PRESS
Portland, Oregon

This revised edition published in North America in 2000 by
Timber Press, Inc.
The Haseltine Building
133 S.W. Second Avenue, Suite 450
Portland, Oregon 97204, U.S.A.

First published in the UK in 1988 by Hamlyn, a division of
Octopus Publishing Group Limited, 2-4 Heron Quays,
London E14 4JP

A catalog record for this book is available from the Library of Congress

ISBN 0-88192-481-4

Produced by Toppan Printing Co., (H.K.) Ltd.
Printed in China

Contents

Foreword

The orchids are an enormous group of plants. Many books have been written about them, over the centuries, but there is still so much to record. The majority of wild orchids are tropical in distribution and there is a great deal to learn about them and their wild habitats. New growers become attracted to their culture every day, but most of the plants need the protection of a greenhouse in temperate climes. Completely new orchids are appearing all the time as so many growers are fascinated by the novelties they can create by hybridisation. Some of the newer hybrids and cultivars present quite different challenges to growers. So I welcome the opportunity to revise this book which first appeared in 1988.

This second edition follows a pattern prescribed for a series of introductory gardening books about special groups of plants at the Royal Botanic Gardens, Kew, UK. Most of the text remains unchanged, but dates and figures have been brought up to date and a few small additions have been made. The bibliography has been rewritten because so many good new books have appeared recently and I want to draw attention to some of these. Also some of the books listed in the first edition may now be hard to find.

I have not altered any of the generic names that were used in the first edition but should point out that botanists have proposed some changes recently. In particular, two species of *Brassavola* (*B. digbyana* and *B. glauca*) are often put in *Rhyncholaelia* now, and *Cirrhopetalum* is often combined with *Bulbophyllum*. The *Lemboglossum* species in this book (formerly in *Odontoglossum*) have been transferred to *Rhynchostele*. The publication of other changes among the genera related to *Oncidium* and *Cattleya* may be imminent. Retaining the familiar names for these orchids, at least for the time being, makes understanding the hybrid names and their derivation much easier. Finally, I have not transferred *Orchis morio* and *Orchis papilionacea* to *Anacamptis* and hope that further DNA studies will reveal that they should remain in *Orchis*.

I hope this small book about a huge subject will stimulate the interest of many newcomers to orchids. Perhaps readers may discover where to look for them in the wild, how to propagate them at home, and how to maintain them for pleasure. Above all I hope that it will inspire people to take up growing orchids, species and hybrids, as a hobby. Anyone who does so will gain many hours and years of interest and delight. A lifetime is not long enough to learn everything about these intriguing plants.

Joyce Stewart
Wisley

Opposite: *Lycaste suaveolens* drawn by W.E. Trevithick, lithograph prepared by Lilian Snelling; depicted in Curtis's *Botanical Magazine,* plate 9231, in 1931 as *Lycaste aromatica* (see page 94)

Introduction

Orchids have been described as the 'royal family' of plants. Anyone who becomes captivated by their intriguing flowers, exciting colours, varied shapes and great diversity of growth habits would certainly agree that they are rather special plants. In numbers of species the Orchidaceae is the largest family in the plant kingdom. Reliable estimates suggest that a figure in the region of 25,000 might include all the wild species currently known. To these can be added over 100,000 artificial hybrids made by growers throughout the world, a figure that is being added to by new crosses every day.

Wild orchids occur throughout the world wherever plant life can flourish. There are many more among the mountains of the tropics than in temperate regions, but seven have even been recorded within the Arctic Circle. Orchids are perennial plants, mostly herbaceous, though a few are vines. More than half the known species grow as epiphytes, clinging to the surface of another plant, a tree or shrub, and deriving their nutrients from substances dissolved in the rainwater that seeps by. Obviously this can be a stressful habitat if no rain falls for several months, and orchids have special vegetative features – swollen stems called pseudobulbs, succulent leaves, and aerial roots with a thick protective and absorptive covering – to help them survive. But it is for their fascinating flowers that orchids are grown and appreciated by many millions of people throughout the world. Every orchid flower is alike in that it has six parts – three coloured sepals, two petals and a third, specialized petal called the lip – surrounding the reproductive parts, which are embedded in the central column. There is so much variation, however, in size and shape, design and decoration, colour, scent and texture, that every orchid flower is different. Here lies their great attraction for anyone interested in growing decorative plants: their incredible diversity, their long-lasting flowers and their adaptability to cultivation are unrivalled.

This book about orchids and orchid-growing begins with the story of the first introductions of orchids to horticulture in the West, more than 250 years ago. The difficult days of learning how to grow them were followed by a huge expansion of interest in their importation and cultivation. Today, the majority of the trade in plants and cut flowers is in the exotic, colourful and reliable man-made hybrids, though some specialists still favour the wild species.

The main part of this book is an overall guide to orchid-growing in temperate regions. The principles of orchid-growing depend on observations of how and where orchids grow in the wild and the environmental conditions they experience there. Methods of emulating or interpreting these conditions in cultivation are considered and recommended. One or more greenhouses are desirable for many of the species, but for others a conservatory or windowsill is adequate. There is a brief look at the orchids that come from cooler parts of the world and will survive in different parts of the garden, and at a few which make good container plants for the patio or terrace in summer. Finally, a selection of the most popular species and hybrids to grow is presented in the A to Z section beginning on page 68.

Opposite: *Disa uniflora* (see page 88)

1
The History and Conservation of Orchids

The worldwide interest in orchids and orchid-growing has been increasing rapidly during the last fifty years, but it is not new. There have been other periods in the past when this activity has been something of a cult. Orchids have been grown for perhaps 3000 years in China: native plants are still tended carefully in pots, and appreciated for their foliage throughout the year as well as for their fragrance when in flower. Greek botanists understood the medicinal value of some of their native species in 300 BC or thereabouts. Shakespeare wrote of the folklore related to the early purple orchid, *Orchis mascula*. The interest in growing tropical orchids in Europe became possible when trade with distant lands began to expand; strange plants and animals were collected and brought home from far-reaching explorations. It is of interest to review, briefly, the major events of the development of orchid-growing in these last 300 years.

EARLY ATTEMPTS AT GROWING ORCHIDS

The first record of cultivated tropical orchids in Europe shows two species growing in Holland at the end of the 17th century. They were illustrated in the book *Paradisus Batavus*, by the Dutch botanist Paul Herman, which was published posthumously in 1698. The American orchid *Brassavola nodosa* (*Epidendron corassavicum*) was figured from a plant flowering in the garden of Casper Fagel (1634–85), and was presumably introduced from Curaçao before 1685. The other illustration is of *Habenaria* (*Pecteilis*) *susannae* (as *Orchis amboinensis*), copied from an illustration sent to him from Ambon by Rumphius, who had named it *Flos susannae* after his wife.

In England the first tropical orchids were seen a little later. In 1732 *Bletia purpurea* flowered in Sir Charles Wager's garden in Fulham; the plant had been imported the previous year from the Bahamas by the cloth merchant Peter Collinson. Phillip Miller recorded several species surviving at Chelsea for a short time in 1768, including a *Vanilla* and some *Epidendrum* species. In about 1778 Dr John Fothergill introduced two terrestrial orchids, *Phaius tankervilleae* and *Cymbidium ensifolium*, from China, the first of which flowered that same year. Records at the Royal Botanic Gardens at Kew show that two American epiphytes, *Encyclia fragrans* and *E. cochleata*, flowered there for the first time in 1787. Aiton's *Hortus Kewensis* enumerated 15 species of exotic orchids in cultivation at Kew in 1789, and more than 70 species in the second edition published in 1813. Some plants were brought to England with great care. There is a record of an *Oncidium* flowering throughout the voyage from Montevideo in Uruguay to England, hung up in the cabin. Others came by accident. *Cattleya labiata* allegedly came first as packing material in a parcel of exotic plants from Brazil, from which it flowered in 1818.

Opposite: *Cattleya labiata* growing wild in Brazil (see also page 77)

These tentative beginnings were made possible by the existence of orangeries in northern Europe, many of which had been built in the 17th century to provide shelter for citrus trees during the winter months. Hot air was circulated through hollow walls and passages, but this produced a dry atmosphere more suitable for cacti and succulents than orchids, though the orange trees survived. The first attempts at cultivating orchids under these conditions were disastrous. Whether they were planted in earth, rotten leaves and wood, or bark, or simply hung up in the dry atmosphere, all died within a few months of their introduction. Many of the tropical epiphytes had been described to the Swedish botanist Linnaeus as growing on trees, so when he named them he used the word *parasitica* in his brief description. Thus a number of growers came to believe that the problem lay in the lack of suitable supporting trees in these hothouses! The high losses did not deter growers from trying more and more foreign orchids as they became available, but success in keeping them alive was slow to arrive. Sir Joseph Hooker (1817–1911), when Director of the Royal Botanic Gardens, Kew, described England at that time as 'the grave of tropical orchids'.

Refinements in growing techniques were gradually adopted, however. Hanging baskets were used for epiphytic orchids by several enthusiasts including Sir Joseph Banks (1744–1820), the botanical adviser to George III, who had several greenhouses at Isleworth. Filled with vegetable compost and covered with moss to support the plant, these baskets were plunged into a tub of water several times a day. Dean Herbert of Manchester (1778–1847) and others grew some of their orchids attached to pieces of bark or wood, and treated them similarly. The Horticultural Society of London (now the Royal Horticultural Society) built up a collection of epiphytes in its greenhouses at Chiswick in order to discover the best methods of cultivating them. This study led their Assistant Secretary in 1830, John Lindley, to present a paper recommending a regime for successful cultivation. This was satisfactory for the species from hot tropical forests at low altitudes, but spelt death to the numerous species from montane areas. Everyone followed his advice, and orchids continued to die. However, Lindley received correspondence from many collectors about the natural habitats of orchids and the climatic conditions where they grew, and published this information in his writings in the *Botanical Register* and in the *Gardeners' Chronicle*, which he founded in 1845. Lindley also published several important descriptive books on classification, many aspects of which are accepted still today. For these contributions he is often referred to as the father of orchidology.

Gradually, as they experimented with growing conditions, the gardeners of the 19th century began to realize that different conditions were necessary for different orchids. One of the first attempts to grow orchids at lower temperatures was made by Joseph Cooper, who was gardener to Earl Fitzwilliam at Wentworth in Yorkshire. He initiated the use of ventilation and the system of 'damping down' of orchid houses, i.e. raising the humidity by regularly watering the floor and benching, thus lowering the temperature as the moisture evaporates. Syringing the plants to imitate a fine mist was tried out by J.C. Lyons in Ireland, and described in his privately printed *Orchid Growers' Manual*, probably the first publication of its kind. Changing the system of heating to steam or pipes filled with hot water provided gentle artificial heat in the greenhouses, which may have been the most significant factor. These details of a new approach to orchid-growing were described in 1851 in a series of articles in the *Gardeners' Chronicle* by Benjamin Williams, together with information on the provenance of orchids and their individual cultural requirements. They formed the basis of the first edition of *The Orchid Grower's Manual* in 1852, which was enormously successful and helpful.

In the second half of the 19th century many thousands of orchids were successfully introduced and grown. By the time the seventh edition of William's book was published in 1894, by his son B.S. Williams, it had expanded from 108 to 796 pages. It is still of great value today, and some of the illustrations for the seventh edition, which has been reprinted many times, are reproduced in this book. A similar publication was Veitch's *A Manual of Orchidaceous Plants*, which appeared in ten parts between 1887 and 1894. At about this time a number of other fine publications appeared, many of them with hand-coloured plates and all illustrating the variety of orchids that were becoming available and giving details of their successful cultivation. *Curtis's Botanical Magazine* had always included a high proportion of orchids among its plant portraits, and continued to do so, particularly during the editorship of Sir Joseph Hooker (1865–1904), for they were one of his favourite groups of plants.

ORCHIDS FROM SEED

The next step forward in orchid cultivation can be related to the flowering, in 1856, of the first artificially produced hybrid orchid, *Calanthe* Dominyi. It was named by Dr John Lindley in honour of the grower John Dominy, who looked after the orchids for the firm of Veitch and Sons at Exeter and later at Chelsea. Not only was this the first of a long line of hybrids, which are still being produced today in ever-increasing sizes and variety of colours, but it demonstrated that orchids could be raised from seed like any other plant.

The structure of the column of the orchid flower and the significance of the various parts for reproduction had been elucidated by Robert Brown. To obtain seeds the pollinarium must be removed from the column of the male parent and transferred to the stigma on the column of the female parent. Provided that the parents are compatible, the pollinated column will begin to swell as pollen tubes grow through it to the ovary. The capsule also begins to swell as fertilization occurs, and it continues to do so as the seeds develop. Ripening may take a few weeks, several months, or as long as a year. At maturity the capsule splits to release millions of tiny dust-like seeds.

The first orchid seedlings were described by R.A. Salisbury in 1802, but raising seedlings took over 50 years to become a popular and widespread method of obtaining new plants. Dean Herbert described in 1847 how he had raised seedlings of *Bletia*, *Cattleya*, *Herminium* and *Ophrys*, and predicted that some startling hybrids might be obtained by someone who could devote enough attention to looking after the young plants. In 1849 David Moore, Curator of the Botanical Gardens, Glasnevin, Dublin, recorded that seedlings of several epiphytic orchids, including epidendrums and *Cattleya forbesii*, had been raised at Glasnevin in the preceding five years, but that keeping them alive during the first five years of their existence was very difficult.

The early methods of raising seedlings were indeed unreliable and met with very limited success. Seeds were sprinkled on the surface of the growing medium around established plants, often one of the parents. Great care was necessary to keep the compost moist, but never saturated. Some success was achieved and the seedlings were removed and potted separately as soon as they were large enough to handle. To increase the numbers raised, James O'Brien, who was Secretary of the Orchid Committee of the Royal Horticultural Society for many years, recommended the use of a propagating case within the greenhouse in which the seeds and seedlings could have sheltered, extra care. As a surface for sowing the seeds he suggested a square of coarse calico or muslin stretched over a ball of sphagnum moss which was then pressed into a small flower pot so that its convex surface was level with the rim of the pot. Squares of soaked *Osmunda* fibre and discs of soft wood such as willow, cut across the grain and wedged in flower pots, were also recommended as germinating surfaces. Fresh seeds germinated readily to form little green, spherical bodies, but between this stage and the young rooted plantlets a year or so later there were many losses.

The first major advance in seed germination and establishment came as a result of the researches of a French botanist, Noel Bernard. In a series of papers begun in 1899 he demonstrated that in the wild orchid seeds germinate in the presence of a mycorrhizal fungus. He next proceeded to show that a symbiotic method of germination could be carried out artificially. Later, work by the German mycologist Hans Burgeff described in great detail how orchid seeds could be germinated *in vitro* on an agar medium containing ground salep (*Orchis* tuber extract) provided that a suitable fungus was present. Furthermore, different orchids had a requirement for a different and particular fungus. This method was eagerly adopted by a number of growers. The numbers of orchids in cultivation, and of hybrid cattleyas and odontoglossums in particular, increased greatly as a result of its use.

It was superseded, and the foundations for the modern techniques of germination and seedling culture were laid, by the work of the American Lewis Knudson in the 1920s. He argued that the action of the fungus in the medium devised by Burgeff would be to convert the starch in the salep (27 per cent of its mass) into simple sugars that could be utilized by the orchid. His experiments duly showed that the fungus was unnecessary provided that the right proportions of essential mineral nutrients and sugars were present in the agar. By 1930 he had successfully germinated seeds and grown the seedlings to flowering size by this method. It has now been adopted, with minor modifications of the formula, throughout the world. The propagation of orchids, whether species or hybrids, from seed has been immensely simplified and increased greatly in quantity as a result.

A further laboratory procedure that has evolved directly from Knudson's method and has promoted another major change in orchid-growing is the application of tissue culture techniques to propagation. Meristem culture and the multiplication of clones by frequent division of the propagules in culture was demonstrated by Georges Morel in 1960. Its widespread adoption has led to an enormous increase in the number of plants in cultivation, and a consequent reduction in their price. These new techniques have had particular significance in the propagation of individual clones that are particularly desirable, either because they have flowers of unusual colour or award quality or because their flowering

Calanthe Veitchii
(*C. rosea* × *C. vestita*) an early
hybrid illustrated
by W. Fitch for
Curtis's *Botanical Magazine*, plate
5375, in 1863 (see
page 76)

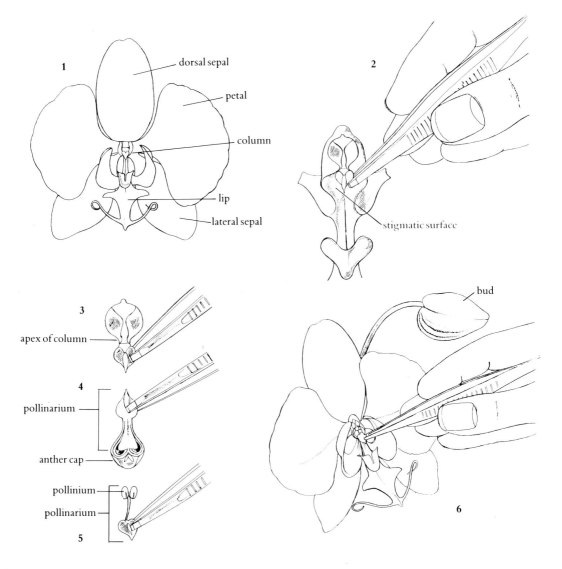

1. dorsal sepal
   petal
   column
   lip
   lateral sepal

2. stigmatic surface

3. apex of column

4. pollinarium
   anther cap

5. pollinium
   pollinarium

6. bud

1. Parts of the flower of *Phalaenopsis amabilis*; **2**. The column viewed from below; **3**, **4** and **5**. Dissections of the column to show the pollinium; **6**. Placement of pollinarium on stigma of another flower

can be controlled precisely to meet heavy seasonal demand. Joseph Arditti has provided excellent reviews of the methods of orchid propagation from tissue culture (1977) and seeds (1982) in *Orchid Biology: Reviews and Perspectives I* and *II*.

HYBRIDIZING

The removal of the pollinarium from one flower and its deposition on the stigma of another is such a simple process, and so easily accomplished with a toothpick, matchstick or needle, that it seems surprising it was not carried out until the 1840s. Dean Herbert hybridized a few orchids in 1846, as well as a number of new bulbs and other plants in his garden. In 1853 the possibility of hybridization was suggested to Veitch's orchid grower, John Dominy, by an Exeter surgeon, John Harris, who demonstrated how to carry out the necessary transfer. Dominy's first cross was between two species of *Cattleya* (*C. guttata* × *C. loddigesii*). This was successful, but the progeny flowered a little later than the less spectacular *Calanthe* Dominyi (*C. furcata* × *C. masuca*), which therefore holds the record of being the first hybrid orchid raised by man to flower. It flowered for the first time in October 1856. The inflorescence was shown to Lindley, who named it after its creator; realizing the potential for hybridizing in the orchid family and the nomenclatural implications this might have, he exclaimed: 'You will drive the botanists mad!'

The first *Cattleya* hybrid to flower was named *C. hybrida*, and although it did not survive for long after flowering the cross has since been remade many times. One of the most famous and still sought after early hybrids was *Paphiopedilum* Harrisianum (*P. villosum* × *P. barbatum*). It flowered in 1869, and commemorates the name of the surgeon who first showed Dominy how feasible orchid hybrids might be. Plants raised from the original cross are still in cultivation more than 130 years later. When part of the Veitch nursery moved to Chelsea in 1864 Dominy went too, and by the time he retired in 1880 he had raised 25 orchid hybrids. His pioneering work had put Messrs Veitch in the forefront of the field. His successor, John Seden, raised 500 hybrids in the next 25 years. Both he and Dominy crossed species of the same genus and those of closely related genera. Some of the latter were tentatively recorded under made-up names, *Laeliocattleya* and *Sophrocattleya* and so on.

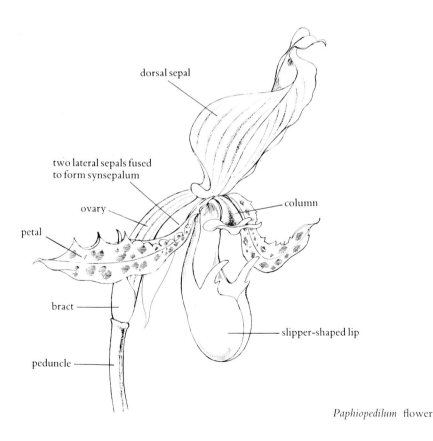

dorsal sepal

two lateral sepals fused to form synsepalum

ovary

column

petal

bract

slipper-shaped lip

peduncle

Paphiopedilum flower

ORCHID NAMES

As more and more hybrids appeared on the scene a new problem arose: how to name and record such mongrel plants? The first list of hybrids compiled by F.W. Burbridge in 1871 had seventeen names. In 1895 Messrs Sander and Sons of St Albans instituted a system for the registration of orchid hybrids and in 1906 published the first issue of *Sander's List of Orchid Hybrids*. This was followed, in 1946, by their *Complete List of Orchid Hybrids*, which contained some 20,000 names and is the starting point for a series still in use today. David Sander published another volume covering registrations between 1946 and 1960, which contained a further 15,000 new hybrids. Since 1961 the registration of orchid hybrids has been managed by the Royal Horticultural Society, and they have published several addenda. The most recent one appeared in 1999, covering the years 1996–98. Lists of new orchid hybrids are published regularly in *The Orchid Review* and other orchid magazines around the world. Hybridists are more active now than ever, and a great many new registrations today come from outside England.

Coining the names for new hybrids soon became a problem, especially when more than one genus was involved. At first parts of the names were blended together. This was easy when two well-known genera were involved; *Laelia* × *Cattleya*, for example, became *Laeliocattleya*. When this was combined with another genus, such as *Brassavola*, the result – *Brassolaeliocattleya* – was a little unwieldy. Very long concoctions could arise if four genera were united. Was the name *Brassolaeliocattlonitis* acceptable for a cross involving *Brassavola* × *Cattleya* and *Laelia* × *Sophronitis*, which was easy to grow and had delightful red or orange

× *Laeliocattleya* Drumbeat 'Triumph' (see page 93)

flowers? For solving this difficulty the orchid world is indebted to the famous gardener E.A. Bowles. He suggested that it would be best to abandon these very long designations where three or more genera were involved, and instead to compose an arbitrary name for such hybrids by adding the termination -*ara* to the name of a person distinguished as a grower or student of orchids. This solution was gratefully accepted, and today we have × *Potinara* (after a French grower, Monsieur Potin) instead of *Sophrolaeliobrassocattleya*; there are many other euphonious and easily recognized names. These intergeneric hybrid names are also recognizable by the × which precedes them.

    In addition to the generic name, the names of orchid hybrids have other components that identify individual plants. This is most easily explained by looking at an example, *Paphiopedilum* Maudiae 'The Queen'. The generic name, *Paphiopedilum*, is printed in italics and with a capital letter, and is sometimes abbreviated to an agreed format, *Paph*. Maudiae is the grex name of a famous green-and-white-flowered slipper orchid. A grex name is similar to the collective name of hybrids in other groups of plants, and is applied to all the progeny raised from two parents that bear the same pair of names, no matter how many times the cross is made. A grex name always begins with a capital letter, is printed in roman type and may consist of one to three words. Cultivar names are used for individual plants (clones) of a particular grex, such as 'The Queen', which has particularly large, well-shaped flowers. Clonal names can be recognized by the fact that they are fancy names of one to three words enclosed in single quotation marks.

Paphiopedilum hybrids showing improvements in size and shape with progressive breeding: left, *P.* Astarte; centre, *P.* F.C. Puddle; right, *P.* Miller's Daughter 'Delilah'

AWARDS TO ORCHIDS

The names of particularly beautiful orchids are often followed by letters such as FCC/RHS or AM/RHS when they are written on labels in plant pots or in nurserymen's catalogues. These letters indicate that the plant has been exhibited to the Orchid Committee of the Royal Horticultural Society and the members of the committee have been sufficiently impressed by it to recommend to the Council of the Society that the plant should be recognized by an award. Two awards are in regular use. The First Class Certificate (FCC) is the highest recognition of horticultural excellence bestowed by the Society. In most years only one or a few FCCs are given to orchids. The Award of Merit (AM) is recommended for plants that are meritorious in some way, and is given much more frequently, particularly to new hybrids. A Preliminary Commendation (PC) is sometimes given to new hybrids, usually young plants, that the Committee would like to see again on a subsequent flowering before committing themselves to a recommendation for a higher award.

This system of awards to outstanding orchids has been operating in England since 1889. At first many awards were given to newly introduced species, but man-made hybrids later received most of the recognition, as they still do today. The system has been copied or adapted in many parts of the world and there are now over 40 award-giving bodies, notably the American Orchid Society (AOS). This practice of recognition by knowledgeable people for noteworthy plants and flowers has always been a great stimulus to growers and hybridizers. Awarded plants have higher commercial value than others, and are frequently used as parents in the breeding of new lines.

CONSERVATION OF ORCHIDS

During the early years of orchid-growing in temperate regions the collection and importation of tropical plants was a necessary prerequisite. Collectors were sent on special expeditions, often at considerable expense, and enormous numbers of plants were shipped back to Europe. Many perished *en route*. Others survived, and changed hands at exorbitant prices in the salerooms of several of the larger cities. They provided the parental stock for the colourful hybrids that are now admired and grown in large numbers.

In the last 40 years a new awareness of a need for conservation has developed among orchid lovers as well as in others interested in wild plants and animals. Orchid growers have realized that the numbers of plants in the wild are finite, that their exploitation must be subject to controls, and that greater efforts should be made to propagate species as well as hybrids from seed. Botanic gardens and the owners of large private collections share a duty to propagate from the stocks they hold. The production and distribution of seeds is encouraged, and several centres are involved in this activity.

Another conservation measure for orchids, as well as other specialized plants that are in demand for horticulture such as cacti, palms and pitcher plants, is the control of international trade. In Washington in 1973 a treaty known as CITES – the Convention on International Trade in Endangered Species of Wild Fauna and Flora – was prepared, and it came into effect in July 1975. More than 140 countries have now approved, accepted or ratified this treaty. It provides for the control of trade simply by the issue of export permits, by a competent management authority in each country, which indicate that international trade in any listed species will not be detrimental to the survival of the wild populations. The lists of species are known as appendices, and are designed to offer different degrees of protection to wild plants. Two of the appendices include orchids. Appendix I lists all species threatened with extinction that are or may be affected by trade. Many orchids are included in this list, and trade in plants of these species collected from the wild is permitted only under exceptional circumstances. Appendix II contains every other orchid that 'although not necessarily now threatened with extinction may become so unless trade . . . is subject to strict regulation'. Exemptions from these appendices, and from the permit system, include seeds, pollinia, tissue cultures and cut flowers of artificially propagated orchids. Artificial hybrids of orchids may be exported with a recognized certificate of artificial propagation, instead of an export permit. They are subjected to this form of control, even though such trade offers no threat to wild populations, because they are often impossible to distinguish from wild species unless they are in flower. The details of the permit system and of the various authorities in different countries can be obtained from the CITES Secretariat, 15 chemin des Anémones, 1219 Chatelain, Geneva, Switzerland. (e-mail: cites@unep.ch)

These controls have diminished the volume of international trade, largely because of the delays and bureaucracy they impose, particularly for small shipments. However, there is an alarming number of attempts to avoid the controls and smuggle rare plants. If detected these result in the confiscation of plants and sometimes in heavy fines.

A more positive approach to conservation lies in the setting aside of rich native habitats as nature reserves. All plants and animals receive protection in these reserves, but the appeal of orchids is so great that a number of reserves have been demarcated primarily to conserve them. Sometimes plants have been moved from areas scheduled for development into safe sites. Some governments already issue licences to commercial and amateur groups for the rescue of interesting plants in areas where large-scale development is about to occur. Much more could be done to salvage threatened plants in these circumstances.

There are also a few instances of reintroduction to the wild of plants artificially propagated in botanical gardens and by enthusiastic amateur growers. These *ex situ* conservation measures should help to complement the regulation of trade and establishment of reserves. Together such efforts should ensure that there will be wild orchids in wild places for posterity.

2
Orchids in the Wild

Before attempting to grow orchids in the greenhouse or the garden it is extremely helpful to acquire some knowledge of the different ways in which they grow in the wild. Because they are such a large family, distributed throughout almost every part of the globe, orchids have developed a number of different growth forms enabling them to compete with other plants in a wide variety of habitats. There are no truly aquatic orchids, no desert-loving plants (though a few survive on the fringes of deserts in several continents), and no trees or shrubs among their number. But there are orchid plants that can survive heat, strong light, drought, cold, strong winds, salt spray, and many other environmental hazards. In their native habitats they are strong plants, often supremely well adapted to the particular conditions in each individual site, able to withstand natural difficulties and disasters with considerable success. Wherever they are, they need plenty of moisture and the stimulus of increased nutrients during the main growing season in order to produce flowers, fruits and seeds to complete the regular cycle of growth.

TERRESTRIALS

Many species of orchid grow in the ground, like other familiar plants of temperate regions. The details of their growth cycle depend on the prevailing climate. Where winters are cold and frosty and the summers warmer and wet, the orchids begin to develop their leaves in the late winter or spring, flower during the summer months and die down again in the autumn. The species that grow in grasslands, marshes or on mountainsides receive full sunlight, but others prefer a shaded site on a woodland or forest floor. Under the soil surface these terrestrial orchids have one or more tubers, thickened roots or a swollen rhizome, which act as a perennating organ, like a bulb or corm, and from which the new growth will emerge when temperatures begin to rise in the following spring.

In areas with a Mediterranean climate – southern Europe, California, parts of Australia and the Cape province of South Africa – the orchids grow and flower during the wet, mild winter months and die off as the warm, dry summer months begin. Their tubers, or other kinds of storage organ underground, are safe and dormant during the hot, desiccating part of the year.

In the tropical parts of the world terrestrial orchids are sometimes evergreen, particularly in forested habitats where the climate is fairly equable throughout the year. Others have a seasonal growth pattern like those in the temperate regions. They usually produce their leaves and flowers during the rainy season, and these parts die back as the dry season advances. Underground tubers, rhizomes or pseudobulbs ensure their survival during the inclement period. Some produce their flowers very early in the growing season, at the same time as the developing leaves emerge or even before them. Others complete their vegetative growth first and flower later, often towards the end of the rainy season.

Opposite: *Vanda tricolor* (see also page 112)

EPIPHYTES AND LITHOPHYTES

More than half the known orchids have developed an epiphytic mode of life. Derived from two Greek words, *epi-* (upon) and *phyton* (plant), epiphytic means that their roots spread over the surface of another plant, usually a tree or shrub, instead of penetrating the soil. The roots are thick and white because of their special outer covering, known as velamen. This is an extremely absorptive layer, soaking up any available moisture like a sponge. It is also a protective layer. When it dries out the many layers of air-filled cells reflect light and heat and protect the living parts of the roots underneath. Epiphytes are not parasites. There is no connection between their roots and the tissues of the host plant on which they grow. They merely use it as a support, a place on which to perch in a brighter, fresher or less crowded environment than the forest floor. Quite a number of epiphytes are able to colonize a rock surface as successfully as they grow on bark. There are also orchids that always creep over rocks and boulders, or grow in cracks between them; these are often known as lithophytes.

Epiphytes and lithophytes are mostly evergreen and slow-growing. Many of them grow in humid places; some flourish where rainfall is frequent and heavy, but all are accustomed to drying out and to surviving long or short periods of drought. Some have developed swollen stems, called pseudobulbs, which act as water storage organs. They become furrowed or shrivelled as the stored moisture is used up when a dry period is prolonged. Others have succulent or leathery leaves, some of which keep their stomata closed during the heat of the day and open them for gas exchange and moisture loss at night, when temperatures are lower and losses will be less.

Growth patterns of orchid plants:
1. Rhizome of *Cypripedium calceolus*; **2**. Tubers and roots of *Ophrys apifera*; **3**. Hairy roots of *Paphiopedilum villosum*; **4**. Roots of *Cymbidium* confined in a pot; **5**. Aerial roots growing from stem of *Phalaenopsis amabilis*

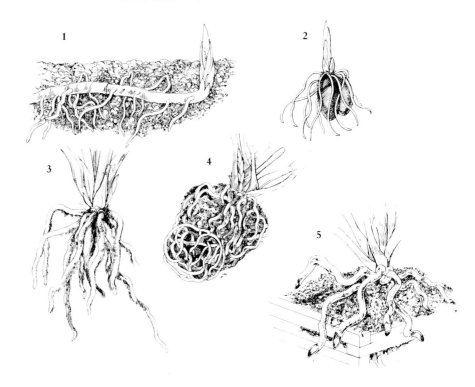

Orchids with
pseudobulbs:
1. *Coelogyne
cristata*;
2. *Dendrobium
crumenatum*;
3. *Cattleya trianaei*

SYMBIOTIC RELATIONSHIP

In the wild many orchids grow in soils or on trees where the availability of
nutrients is low. As seeds and seedlings, and often as adult plants, they overcome
this apparent disadvantage by forming a close association with a symbiotic
fungus. In this mycorrhizal association, as it is known, the orchid provides shelter
to the fungus in the cells of its roots, and in return obtains nutrients that the fungus
has derived from decaying plant and animal fragments in the surrounding litter.
In this way the orchid utilizes the fungus as a kind of extended root system, and
obtains nutrients that would otherwise be unavailable.

DISTRIBUTION

The distribution of orchids, both epiphytes and terrestrials, is affected by the
presence or absence of other vegetation and by the seasonal distribution and
availability of moisture. Where orchids grow is also determined to a large extent
by altitude above sea level, particularly in the tropics. At low altitudes or near the
sea, temperatures are usually high during the day and do not drop much at night.
Further inland, and especially between 900 and 1800 m (about 3000 and 6000 ft)
above sea level, warm days are followed by much cooler nights. At higher
altitudes the days are fresh, as temperatures are lower, and there is a corresponding
drop at night. At the highest altitudes, below the permanent snow cover of the
mountain peaks, the climate has been described as 'summer every day and winter
every night', but even here a few orchids enjoy the isolation and the sunlight.
Different orchid species are to be found in many of these situations. Often a
particular species is restricted to quite a narrow range of conditions. Perhaps the
richest areas of the world are the cool, moist mountain valleys of South America,
but all mountainous areas, with their wide variety of different but interlinked
habitats, are much richer in species than the hot coastal lowlands.

3
The Principles of Orchid Growing

The description in Chapter 2 of the growing conditions of orchid plants in the wild highlighted features that make orchids different from other plants. These must be borne in mind when trying to grow them. The first thing to remember is that there are very many different kinds of orchids, with an almost equally different range of requirements. Learning about each group of species or individuals and what their requirements are is the first step. Finding ways to provide them is the second. Understanding the changes in the needs of orchid plants at different seasons, the importance of alternating periods of wetness and dryness, of light and shade, of growth and resting, will contribute to the successful management of orchid plants in cultivation.

All that is needed for the survival of the species from cool temperate areas is to choose a congenial site in the garden, bearing in mind the natural habitat of each orchid. Orchids that are truly hardy will survive even the hardest winters out of doors without any extra protection.

Several groups of orchids require protection from frost. These include some of the terrestrial orchids from Japan and North America, such as *Calanthe* and *Cypripedium*, and some of the high-altitude plants of the tropical genera, such as *Pleione*. A greenhouse that is also used for alpines, or for propagation during the summer months, will suffice for these during the winter.

ORCHIDS UNDER GLASS

A heated greenhouse or conservatory is a basic necessity for the warmer growing and tropical species. Suitable conditions for a number of different groups of orchids can be provided within a single building, but if it can be subdivided into sections providing different temperatures, a wider selection of orchids can be grown. For the benefit of growers, orchids are often described in cultivation manuals as 'cool', 'intermediate', or 'warm'. This is a shorthand device for referring to the minimum night-time temperature requirements of the different groups, which more or less reflects their altitudinal distribution in the wild.

In the 'cool' house, thermostats are set so that a minimum night-time temperature of 10°C (50°F) is maintained during the winter months. During the summer this is allowed to rise to the ambient temperature, as heating systems are usually switched off. Several different kinds of regimes can be located within the cool house. Cymbidiums require light and airy conditions with relatively low humidity, especially during the winter. Some of the Australian dendrobiums, the cooler growing coelogynes, a few epidendrums and paphiopedilums will also tolerate the environment that suits cymbidiums. The odontoglossums and their allies from Central and South America require more shade and humidity and a low maximum temperature during the summer, preferably not exceeding 25°C (75°F). However, they can be grown together by careful placing of the individual plants, the cymbidiums on the higher shelves, nearer the light and ventilators, and

Opposite: *Cattleya bicolor* from Brazil (see page 78)

the odontoglossums, masdevallias, pleurothallids, and other cool forest epiphytes below them in the shade cast by their leaves and in the extra humidity nearer the floor.

In the 'intermediate' house a great variety of orchids can be grown, and plants from a wide range of habitats including mountainous regions can be accommodated. A minimum night-time temperature of 13–15°C (55–60°F) is maintained during the winter months. All the cattleyas and their allies do well in these conditions, and flower best where there is plenty of light. In the shade cast by their pots and leaves, or on the cooler and darker north side of a greenhouse, all the tropical slipper orchids, both paphiopedilums and phragmipediums, do well. The species and hybrids of *Miltoniopsis* and many species of *Bulbophyllum*, *Coelogyne*, *Encyclia*, *Epidendrum* and *Maxillaria* will also flourish under these conditions.

In the 'warm' house the minimum night-time temperature is at least 18°C (65°F), and should be accompanied by high humidity at all times. The shady side of the house is the best place for *Phalaenopsis* species and hybrids, jewel orchids, *Vanilla*, and other tropical forest species. On the lighter side, and where there is more air movement, the Asiatic vandas and their allies can be grown, together with ansellias and some of the angraecums from Africa. The larger dendrobiums, oncidiums, and the deciduous calanthes grow well in this house during the summer, moving to a cooler house in the autumn.

Drainage and moisture

An important feature for pot-grown orchids lies in the provision of excellent drainage and aeration within the growing medium. Although they are moisture-loving plants, orchids always grow in places where periodic dryness is possible. High up in the trees the epiphytes become saturated in every storm, in enveloping clouds, or in heavy dew at night, but they dry out rapidly and always enjoy a buoyant atmosphere. Good ventilation, or the use of fans to provide constantly moving air, can simulate these natural conditions. Similarly, many terrestrial orchids grow on sloping hillsides, in well-drained grassland, or in the shallow layer of leaf litter on the forest floor. Their roots suffer periodic inundation but dry out quickly. Even the marsh orchids and a few riverside species usually grow where there is movement of water, or where the roots dry out for part of the year.

The key to good drainage is the selection of suitable composts or growing media. Most terrestrial species need a generous quantity of grit in the medium; it is, however, helpful to know as much as possible about the natural habitat. Some species prefer calcareous soils; others are only found in damp, peaty places; and yet others thrive in gravelly soils at the roadside. The epiphytic kinds are nearly always grown in a compost that contains pieces of pine bark, perlag (coarse grade particles of expanded volcanic rock) and charcoal in varying amounts, but some do better when mounted on a piece of timber or cork oak bark so that their roots are truly aerial, as they would be in the wild.

In addition to offering good drainage and aeration for the roots, an orchid compost must also be moisture-retentive. This may seem paradoxical, but in fact is only another example of simulating what happens in nature. Bark, humus and soil retain moisture long after rainwater has percolated away from the orchid roots through the spaces between the various surrounding plants and materials. Humidity is essential, both to prevent desiccation and for the survival of the mycorrhizal fungus, which makes nutrients available for orchid growth. In cultivation orchids are usually grown without associated fungi. The grower must therefore provide extra nutrients, either in the compost or, preferably, in very dilute form when plants are watered. In this way a continuous but small supply is maintained, which the plant can absorb through its roots.

In the artificial environment of a greenhouse it is important to provide water of good quality at appropriate intervals. Rainwater is usually best for orchids, except in areas of industrial pollution. However, tap (potable) water can be perfectly satisfactory in soft water areas where the pH measurement is below 7; a pH of 6–7 is ideal. The local water authority should be able to supply an analysis of the average water quality in a particular area, and also to give advice about the treatment required if the water is unusual in any respect. At Kew, for example, the potable water is hard (containing calcium salts) and heavily chlorinated, and thus is not used because it is deleterious to many orchids.

Odontoglossum crispum (see page 99)

4
Cultivation

Many people begin orchid-growing when they acquire a single plant, often as a present. An orchid plant will grow and flower on a windowsill or among a group of other potted plants in a hall, living room or even a bathroom. The flowers of many of the popular orchids will last for six or eight weeks. When the flowers have faded you will probably want to replace the plant with another in order to extend the pleasure you have had from the first one. If this pattern continues you will soon have a small orchid collection. Then the question of housing them arises. If the number of plants remains small, a windowsill can be used to accommodate them. Very soon, however, the windowsills will be full, and then you will need to find an area where supplementary light can be provided, either in a specially made plant case or in an area set aside in a basement or spare room. If space and funds permit, you may prefer to build a greenhouse, ideally one that can be divided into two or more sections to provide slightly different conditions for the different kinds of orchids. Some growers get great satisfaction from growing only a single genus of orchids, such as the tropical slipper orchids, the masdevallias or the odontoglossums. This greatly simplifies the provision of good growing conditions. In this chapter we look at the facilities and equipment needed for orchid-growing, and some of the special cultural features of these plants in different situations.

WINDOWSILL ORCHIDS

Many of the tropical orchids that have been cosseted in greenhouses in the past will do equally well on a windowsill if a few basic rules are observed. The most important ones are to ensure both that there is enough light for the plants, without too much heat, and also that there is adequate humidity in the immediate surroundings. During the winter months a south-facing windowsill, or a table in the curve of a bay window, is probably the best place in the home for orchids, but this might prove too hot in the summer even when the plants are protected by a sun-filtering curtain. In the summer they are probably best on an east-facing windowsill where they will receive the morning sun. A deep windowsill is ideal, as it can be fitted with a polypropylene tray containing about 2–3 cm (1 in) of Hortag (expanded clay aggregate) or some other clean, moisture-retentive material. If the contents of the tray are kept moist but not waterlogged there will always be a suitably humid atmosphere around the orchid pots placed on top.

There is a wide choice of orchids available for this kind of cultivation. Many homes are probably kept too warm for the cool-growing types to succeed for long, though some of the miniature cymbidiums that are now widely available will flower over many months on a windowsill. They can be put outside in dappled shade for the summer when they are not in flower. As permanent house plants, a choice should be made from among the orchids usually described as intermediate; those with a compact growth habit and tidy root system are ideal.

Opposite: Miniature *Cymbidium* Strathdon 'Cooksbridge Noel' AM/RHS (see page 82)

Some of the paphiopedilums and the smaller-growing cattleyas and their hybrids have a good record as windowsill orchids. Other suggestions are made on page 114.

GROWING UNDER ARTIFICIAL LIGHT

Many people living in studios or flats without a garden grow orchids well in a special area of their homes where extra artificial light can be provided. Sometimes orchids grown in this way are superior to those in a greenhouse, as they can be provided with the same quality of light for 12 hours or more every day, as in the tropics, instead of the short winter days of northern temperate regions.

Fluorescent tubes of the 'warm white' variety are the best source of light. They can be erected in banks of four or more over a growing area of trays containing gravel or charcoal on which the plants are set. The leaf surface of the plant needs to be kept 15-45 cm (6-18 inches) below the lights - nearer will be too hot and further away not light enough. Sometimes a growing area is enclosed in a glass case or a recess, where it is much easier to maintain the best humidity levels for orchids. Specially designed plant cases, in modern or traditional style, can be attractive pieces of furniture and very suitable for paphiopedilums, phalaenopsis and other orchids with low light requirements.

ORCHIDS IN A GREENHOUSE

Many people start with a few orchids mixed with other plants in a very small greenhouse, but this is not ideal. If you are choosing a greenhouse specifically for orchids it is important to remember that small houses are much more difficult to keep cool in summer, without losing some of the essential humidity, than are larger ones. The cost of heating a small structure in winter is proportionally greater because of the large surface area of small greenhouses. For heat conservation it is wise to choose a 'planthouse' type of structure, with solid walls up to the level of the staging, rather than the 'glass-to-ground' style, which is more suitable for tomatoes. The minimum size for efficiency in a small orchid greenhouse is 2.4 m wide by 3 m long (8 ft × 10 ft). If the width can be increased to 3.8 m (12 ft), it will be possible to fit in a centre bench as well as benches along the sides, and many more plants can be accommodated.

Siting a greenhouse for orchid-growing in a small garden can present problems. It will need the maximum amount of light possible during the winter months, so should not be shaded by trees or buildings on the south side. Making provision to shade the greenhouse by artificial means is much more satisfactory than trying to arrange shading from permanent features of the plot or boundary. The orientation of a small greenhouse is not important, but once the collection begins to grow an east-west greenhouse is best. With the longest side of the house facing south, the maximum amount of light will enter during the winter. Similarly, a conservatory for orchid-growing should be on the south side of the house for maximum winter light and warmth. However this will also create very hot conditions in summer, making shading essential. Connecting electricity, heating appliances and water to a conservatory attached to the house is no problem; it may be wise to site a free-standing greenhouse as near as possible to a dwelling for the same reason, and for ease of access during the winter months.

Designing the interior of a greenhouse for orchid-growing can be fun. Tiered staging along the sides increases the amount of space for plants and makes it easier to see those near the back. Space must be allowed to hang epiphytic plants in baskets (and a structure to hang them from) so that they will not drip onto plants underneath. A piece of stout mesh along one end is often a very useful area for hanging small plants. Open staging made of slats of wood or galvanized mesh will promote air circulation around the plants, but it should not be too widely spaced or small pots will fall over. It may be helpful to have a concrete path or stepping stones between the benches, but these should have a rough surface so that they do not become slippery as a result of algal growth in the humid conditions.

Environmental factors

In the wild, orchids grow in competition with other plants, whether in the canopy of trees, among rocks or in open grasslands. An investigation of the details of their environment will reveal the conditions that are best for them in a greenhouse: shading from direct sunlight, temperatures moderate to warm but not excessively high, good drainage, high relative humidity coupled with good air movement, and plenty of rainwater during the growing season. It is not always easy, in a greenhouse, to provide all these features at optimum levels in combination, but it is important to achieve the best possible *balance* of humidity, light, warmth and air movement for healthy growth and maximum flowering. A greenhouse full of plants is usually a well-balanced one, and there are many other plants whose growing requirements are compatible with those of orchids. Begonias, hoyas, columneas, bromeliads, peperomias, ferns and other tropical plants can all find a place in a heated greenhouse and help to provide the right atmosphere. It is helpful to have an earth floor under the benches, in which some of these companion plants will thrive.

Light and shading

Orchids have a wide range of light requirements. Some, such as *Ludisia* and some of the paphiopedilums, grow in the deepest shade of tropical forests; there are others – some of the laelias and encyclias, for example – that grow naturally in full sunlight. By arranging the plants carefully in relation to each other in the greenhouse their individual needs can be met. In temperate regions it is necessary to deal with the considerable seasonal differences in the amount of light available. For part of the year it will be necessary to exclude some of the incident light. This can be achieved in one of two ways, and sometimes both are used. The simplest method is to apply a coat of temporary shading paint for greenhouses to the outside of the glass as soon as the days become appreciably longer and brighter in spring. By early summer this may need to be removed and replaced with a thicker coat. It is also useful to have some form of additional shading over the glass during the four or five brightest summer months. Laths or blinds giving about 50 per cent shade when fitted 20–30 cm (10–12 in) above the glass are ideal. Such shading not only cuts down the amount of light entering the house through the roof but also provides a layer of insulation above the glass, thus helping to keep temperatures inside the house somewhat lower. During the autumn the shading can be removed – first the extra layer over the glass, and then the paint – before winter begins.

A pale variety of
Cattleya skinneri
from Costa Rica
(see page 79)

Heating and cooling

Many orchids can adapt to a wide range of temperature conditions. Keeping up the required night-time temperatures is often a problem only of expense. It is best achieved by using electric fan heaters, stationed so that they do not blow hot air on to the plants, or water-filled pipes warmed by an outside boiler. Conveniently situated greenhouses can be connected to a domestic central heating system.

In many greenhouses, particularly the smaller ones, the main difficulty is not in keeping the house warm enough in winter but in keeping the temperatures down in summer. Some of the cooler-growing orchids, masdevallias and odontoglossums, for example, grow poorly if temperatures rise beyond 25°C (75°F), and all orchids are under stress if the temperature reaches more than 32°C (90°F). These temperatures are easily exceeded inside a small glass structure on a hot summer day. Plenty of ventilation is essential, but opening all the windows and doors can result in a sudden lowering of humidity, which is undesirable. Cooling can be effected by increasing the water content of the air. The well-known practice of 'damping down' by spraying water on the benches and floors, and misting over the plants (with soft water), both increases the humidity inside the house and lowers the temperature. Some form of shading over the outside of the glass also has a cooling effect. Continuously running greenhouse fans are also extremely useful, both for their cooling effect and in keeping the air fresh and buoyant.

Humidity

Most orchids grow where humidity levels are high at night as well as during the day. The optimum relative humidity for most orchids is 65–75 per cent at midday, but for phalaenopsis, vandas and their relatives it can be higher. Damping down several times a day is effective. A more sophisticated system, using a humidistat among the plants to operate an automatic under-bench sprayline, is very useful for those who are away from their plants during the day. Sometimes the humidity is more difficult to regulate during the winter months, especially at night when heating systems are working full-time. Damping down last thing at night is a very useful exercise. Flowers can be enjoyed and nocturnal pests searched for at the same time.

Fresh air

Anyone who has travelled in tropical countries, especially at medium or higher altitudes where orchids grow, will have noticed how comfortable the atmosphere is, despite the temperature and humidity, because of the constant breeze. The need for constant fresh air in the greenhouse cannot be stressed too strongly. Ventilators should be open whenever the outside temperatures are warm enough. This can be arranged automatically by a simple device with thermostatic controls. Fans especially designed for greenhouse use are invaluable. Anyone who has tried to grow orchids without one notices an immediate response in the growth of the plants when a fan is installed.

BASIC CULTIVATION

Containers

Like other pot plants, orchids can be grown in a wide range of containers, but certain types are more suitable than others. As they are slow-growing and long-lived, orchids will need tough and durable containers. If the plants are to be brought into the house as decorative features the containers should also be attractive. The most important feature to bear in mind when choosing containers is good drainage for the plants. It is often necessary to enlarge the holes provided by the manufacturer, using a hole-saw on plastic pots and a hammer on clay ones. Plastic pots are widely used today, and round or square ones are equally satisfactory. They are clean and light to handle, and pots especially made for orchids, with extra drainage holes in the sides, are sometimes available. Clay pots were formerly used, especially in large collections with staff to look after them, but the plants and compost tend to dry out more quickly through their porous surface. Whichever is chosen it is convenient to have either one kind or the other, rather than both in the greenhouse.

Many epiphytes grow well on slabs of cork oak bark. To start with they must be tied firmly to the surface, usually with coarse nylon thread, plastic tape or copper wire, but new roots will soon grow and make them secure. Other orchids do very well, and look most attractive, in slatted teak baskets containing orchid compost within a lining of moss.

Hanging baskets made of wire or wood can also be used. Baskets are essential for orchids like stanhopeas, whose flowers grow straight downwards from the base of the plants and would be hidden in a pot. They also prove convenient containers for orchids with pendulous stems – some of the dendrobiums, for example, or for orchids that have long dangling inflorescences like *Coelogyne dayana*.

Composts

The compost in which orchids are grown has the dual function of supporting the plant in its container and providing the roots with a medium that is well aerated yet moisture retentive. It is seldom replaced more than once a year, and often at longer intervals, so it must decompose slowly. Composts in use today are usually mixtures of natural materials such as pieces of pine or fir bark, coarse grit, fibrous peat, chopped dried leaves or sphagnum, and inert materials like perlite, perlag, pieces of horticultural-grade charcoal and sometimes pieces of polystyrene. Synthetic materials like rockwool, pieces of foam, or mixtures of these, are also used very successfully with odontoglossums, masdevallias and paphiopedilums. Individual growers and nurserymen each have their favourite mixes, which are successful in their own greenhouses and with their different watering regimes. A mix containing large particles with large spaces between them will need more frequent watering than a close mix with particles of small size.

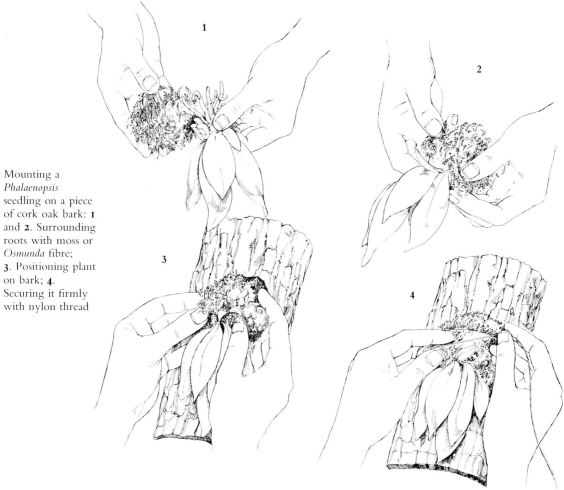

Mounting a *Phalaenopsis* seedling on a piece of cork oak bark: **1** and **2**. Surrounding roots with moss or *Osmunda* fibre; **3**. Positioning plant on bark; **4**. Securing it firmly with nylon thread

Many growers add bone meal, dried blood or hoof and horn meal to these mixtures when plants are potted. Others prefer a compost that is completely inert so that they can supply known quantities of fertilizer to the plants as a dilute feed on a regular basis throughout the growing season.

Two tried and tested compost mixes are given below; they can be modified to suit individual orchids.

Basic epiphyte mix
3 parts washed bark chips, medium grade
1 part coarse perlag
1 part charcoal, horticultural grade
1 part fibrous peat or broken leaves or chopped sphagnum

Basic mix for terrestrial orchids
3 parts fibrous peat
2 parts coarse perlite
2 parts coarse grit
1 part charcoal, horticultural grade

Potting
Choosing the right size of pot is the first essential when potting an orchid. Its roots need to have ample space within the container, and allowance should be made for a year's growth, but overpotting is detrimental. Too much compost can cause poor drainage, and weak roots need to be restricted until the plant has grown healthy new ones. Many orchids do best in rather small pots. To ensure that drainage is efficient the container is often filled one-third full with pieces of polystyrene, crock or large stones. The latter are particularly useful in plastic pots as the extra weight provides greater stability.

The technique of potting is simple. The plant is held in the pot with one hand so that the crown of the plant, the base of the pseudobulbs, or the part of the plant from which the roots emerge is just below the level of the rim. Compost is filled in around the roots with the other hand and gently shaken into the spaces between them by tapping the pot gently on the bench several times. Small plants or those with a poor root system may need to be tied to a stake, a short piece of cane or stiff wire, until they become established.

For ease of handling, growers usually pot orchids into a dry compost and then water it thoroughly, sometimes on two or three consecutive days, to make sure that the constituents are completely moistened. Newly potted plants are then not watered again for two or three weeks to allow the roots to settle. During this time the plants must be kept in a humid place and misted over frequently to make sure that the leaves do not become desiccated.

Repotting
Orchid plants need repotting from time to time. After a good season they may begin to grow over the edge of the pot, or root growth may be so good that they are pushed up out of the pot. Large plants may need dividing or potting on into a larger container. Plants that have died off in the middle or on one side may need to be rejuvenated. The most common reason for repotting is that the compost has

× *Ascocenda* Yip
Sum Wah 'Tilgates'
AM/RHS (see page
71)

deteriorated. If there is difficulty getting a well-grown plant out of the old pot, it is sometimes helpful to leave it in a bucket of water for an hour or two. The saturated plant then slides out easily.

During repotting all the old compost is removed and discarded. Dead roots, which are soft and brown, should be removed carefully as near as possible to the base. It is a good idea to use sterile tools for this operation in order to avoid spreading virus and other diseases. Healthy roots will be white, and should be damaged as little as possible. They are rather brittle, but if they crack no harm will be done. Without compost and with clean healthy roots, the plant can then be carefully examined for any sign of scale insects, treated if necessary, and divided or reshaped as required. Old, leafless pseudobulbs can be removed for propagation before the tidy plant is repotted in a clean pot with fresh compost, as described above.

Some orchids resent disturbance and take a long time to re-establish after repotting. For some of the larger orchids in the *Vanda* alliance, including the angraecums, repotting is rarely necessary, as very coarse bark pieces are used in the compost mix and these take a long time to deteriorate unless the plants are frequently overwatered.

Mounted plants on bark slabs may not need further attention for many years. If they become loose it may be desirable to transfer them to a fresh mount. Sometimes a thick growth of moss develops around mounted plants, and this may need to be removed from time to time to make sure the roots do not lack air.

Watering and spraying

All orchid plants need to dry out. Some need to do so every day, others over a longer period such as a week, while others grow best with a long, moist growing season followed by a dry period of several months. The best approach for the new grower is to try to find out as much as possible about the natural habitat of the different kinds of orchids and find ways of imitating the wild environment in the management of the greenhouse. For a pot plant grower, the hardest part in the transition to becoming an orchid grower is learning not to overwater the plants. Rainwater is best, but it should be stored in a dark tank in the greenhouse so that it stays clean and is at the right temperature for the plants.

After repotting plants will need very little water in the pot because their roots are inactive. Swamping them at this stage may damage such roots as remain. During a period of a month or two the plants' moisture needs can be met by spraying or misting over the leaves, early in the day or, on sunny days, several times during the day. It is best to make sure that moisture does not lodge in leaf axils or the apex of new shoots overnight when temperatures drop, as the recently established plants may be more susceptible to water-borne disease. Misting over the leaves is always a useful exercise on sunny days, as it helps to ensure high humidity in the greenhouse and also lowers the leaf temperature.

Once the plants are properly established in their pots or baskets and new root growth is visible, a regular watering regime can begin. On each occasion plants should be heavily and thoroughly watered, so that the compost is really wetted. If a hose is used it is helpful to fit a water breaker to it, or to use a watering lance with a fine rose. This ensures a gentle flow of water so that the loose compost is not washed out of the pot.

Dendrobium williamsonii from Thailand (see page 85)

How often watering should be carried out will depend on the size of the pot and the kinds of compost used, as well as on the weather. There is really no substitute for daily inspection of the plants. The need for water can often be assessed by the weight of the pots once one becomes used to handling them. Once or twice a week is a good routine, but daily watering may be necessary in

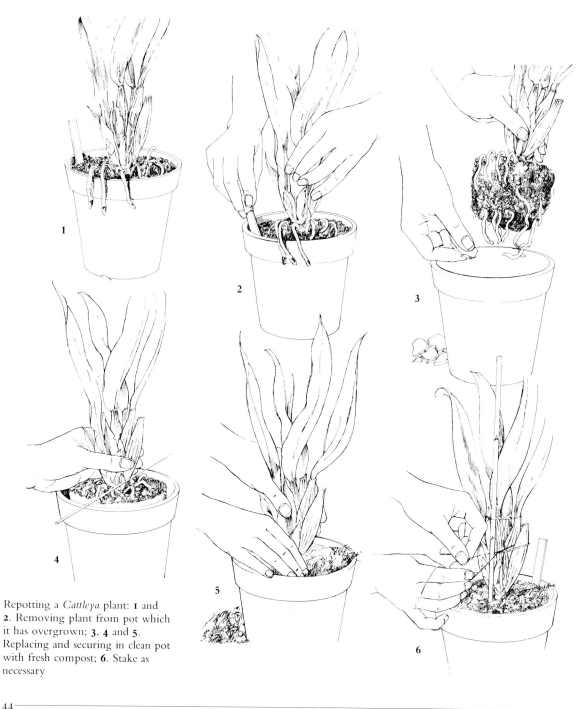

Repotting a *Cattleya* plant: **1** and **2**. Removing plant from pot which it has overgrown; **3**, **4** and **5**. Replacing and securing in clean pot with fresh compost; **6**. Stake as necessary

summer. During the winter watering is usually reduced to once every week or two, and for a few plants water is given only monthly. Some people prefer to water their plants early in the day so that the foliage will have dried off by nightfall when temperatures drop. Others observe that in the tropical habitats of many orchids, storms arise at midday or in the afternoons and the plants are frequently still wet at night.

Feeding

Because orchid composts are relatively inert, the plants will greatly benefit from being fed during their growing season. A dilute liquid fertilizer is the most convenient form to use as it can be applied during watering. Many of the proprietary brands of liquid fertilizer are suitable, but they need to be diluted to quarter or half the strength that is recommended for other pot plants. Little and often is a good maxim, but only when the plant is in active growth. Foliar feeding is sometimes recommended, but bear in mind that uptake through the leaves is rather limited.

Many growers prefer to use a high nitrogen fertilizer (30:10:10) early in the summer to encourage maximum growth while temperatures are high and days are long. Once the growths have matured, it is a good idea to change for a month or two to a fertilizer that will encourage flowering, such as some of those sold for tomato crops, which are high in potash (10:10:30). For the rest of the year a balanced fertilizer (10:10:10) should be used. Other growers prefer to use natural fertilizers, such as chicken manure or a liquid feed prepared from seaweeds. Great care must be taken to ensure that whatever is used is sufficiently dilute or the orchid roots can be damaged.

Resting

Many terrestrial orchids undergo a long dormant season, when their pseudobulbs or tubers wait underground until favourable conditions for growth return. The season may be hostile because it is either too hot or too cold, but most commonly 'resting' is used to overcome drought. The epiphytic orchids are also structurally adapted to withstand a dry period. This often coincides with lower temperatures. Except for the species that grow in swamps or in equatorial forests, where some rain falls in every month, orchids need to dry out or 'rest' at some stage during their annual growth cycle.

In cultivation this need must not be forgotten. It is no use continuing to give water and fertilizer to dormant plants, and it may actually be harmful. The resting period may last for only a few weeks, for example with the Indian dendrobiums, in which its start is signalled by the withering of leaves and its end by the development of new shoots. As soon as a new pseudobulb begins to grow, the plant should be watered freely again.

For many Mexican orchids, especially those that grow at high altitude, the dry season lasts for several of the winter months and plants often flower during this period. The days are short and, with less light and lower temperatures, growth is minimal. Nevertheless, in cultivation plants must be maintained in a humid environment, particularly at night, or they will become too desiccated. If the leaves begin to fall or the pseudobulbs become wrinkled, a little water can safely be given.

5
Propagation

A cheap and interesting way of increasing an orchid collection involves propagation from the plants you already have. Duplicates are always useful as gifts or to exchange with other enthusiasts. They can be produced very easily by division of mature plants, by propagation from dormant buds on 'backbulbs', by taking cuttings of various kinds, and by hand pollinating the plants to obtain seeds. Each of these techniques is somewhat specialized, and they will be reviewed briefly below.

DIVISIONS AND BACKBULBS

Large plants are easily divided into two or more parts when they are repotted. Sometimes a plant will literally fall apart into several pieces. Other plants have pseudobulbs that are joined to each other by a tough rhizome, which needs to be cut with a sterile knife or secateurs. It is a mistake to make too many divisions in the interests of rapid multiplication as the plants may then be too small to survive. For most orchids two or three growths should be retained in each division.

Opposite: *Paphiopedilum* Winston Churchill (see page 104) **Left**: *Masdevallia* Kimballiana (see page 96)

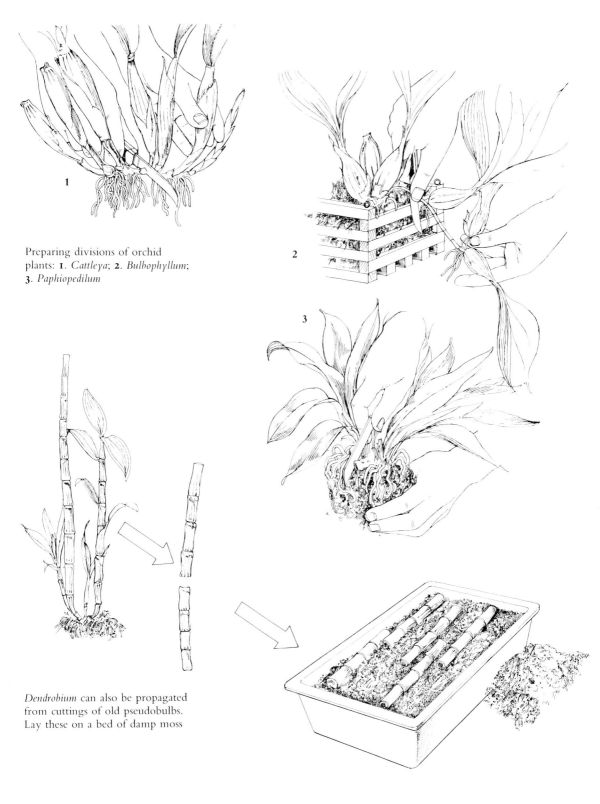

Preparing divisions of orchid
plants: **1**. *Cattleya*; **2**. *Bulbophyllum*;
3. *Paphiopedilum*

Dendrobium can also be propagated
from cuttings of old pseudobulbs.
Lay these on a bed of damp moss

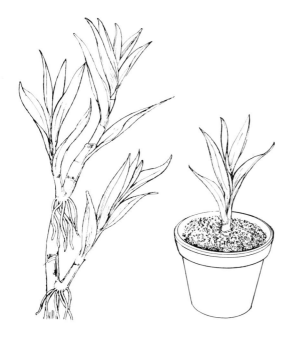

Plantlets or 'keikis':
on a *Dendrobium*
pseudobulb.
Remove and pot
up for propagation

Cattleyas and their allies need at least one leafy pseudobulb on the back growth, with a prominent dormant bud at its base, to have a good chance of success. For lycastes and members of the odontoglossum alliance two or three pseudobulbs are usually separated together. Cymbidiums are the easiest to propagate, from old, leafless pseudobulbs removed from the back of the plant. All loose sheaths should be removed, and the cut base of each pseudobulb allowed to dry. It can then be inserted up to a third of its height in sharp sand or grit and kept moist in a cool corner of the greenhouse. Within two or three months a new shoot will appear above the surface. After a further two or three months the shoot will have its own roots and can be potted up, preferably with the old pseudobulb attached for the first year. New plants propagated in this way may reach flowering size in two or three years.

CUTTINGS

The pseudobulbs, stems and inflorescence stalks on some orchids make suitable propagating material when they are divided into cuttings. Each section must contain one or more dormant buds, and when it is detached from the rest of the plant and kept in suitably humid surroundings, such as being laid on a bed of damp moss or inserted in a pan of moist grit, these buds will form new plantlets. After a few months they can be removed from the old piece of plant and potted up individually. The cane-like stems of epidendrums and dendrobiums yield new plants in this way. The basal parts of the inflorescence stalks of phalaenopsis, phaius and calanthes also have a few dormant buds, each of which will make a new plantlet under appropriate conditions. On many pseudobulbs, dormant buds will occasionally develop little plants, sometimes known as 'keikis', quite spontaneously. These can be removed and potted up as soon as they have a few roots to support their independent growth.

NEW PLANTS FROM SEEDS

Orchid seeds are extremely small. They consist of a tiny embryo surrounded by a single layer of protective cells. They are so small that the food reserves in the embryo are inadequate, by themselves, for the early development of the new plant. In nature most orchid seeds begin life in a partnership with a symbiotic fungus. The fungal hyphae, which are present in the soil or on the bark of a host tree, invade the seed and enter the cells of the embryo. The orchid soon begins to digest the fungal tissue and obtain nutrients from it, thus using the fungus as an intermediary in obtaining nutrients from decaying material in the soil.

In the laboratory this process can be imitated by sowing sterilized seeds with portions of the fungus on a suitable jelly-like medium called agar containing porridge oats, which the fungus can utilize. A simpler method is to use a medium containing all the mineral nutrients, water and sugar that the germinating seed needs and dispense with the fungus. All these techniques must be carried out in conditions as sterile as an operating theatre; otherwise it is extremely easy for the nutrient medium to become infected with unwanted micro-organisms, which develop at the expense of the orchid. The work can be carried out in the kitchen, using a domestic pressure cooker to prepare sterile glassware and media. A sterile box or even a large polythene bag can be used as a cover for the operation, which should be carried out as speedily as possible. However, it is much easier, and success is more assured, if the technique is carried out in a specialized laboratory.

Conical flasks or sterile bottles containing the newly sown seeds are kept under controlled conditions while the embryo grows out through the seedcoat to form,

Opposite:
Dendrobium crumenatum seedlings on a tree trunk in Singapore Botanic Gardens
Right: *Laelia lobata* from Brazil (see page 92)

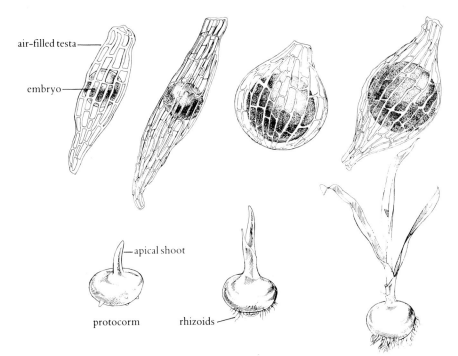

air-filled testa

embryo

apical shoot

protocorm

rhizoids

Germination: seeds
of various shapes
with developing
embryo and,
below from left to
right, the
protocorm at
various stages of
development

first, a rounded protocorm covered in rhizoids, and then a small plantlet.
Sometimes the containers need to be kept in the dark for the first few months, but
the epiphytic orchids develop green protocorms almost immediately and are kept
under artificial light for 12–16 hours each day. After a few months, although the
flasks are sealed, the medium becomes too solid through dehydration and the
plantlets need to be transferred to freshly prepared medium in a new container.
These techniques must also be carried out under sterile conditions. Eventually,
about six to twelve months after sowing, the plantlets are large enough to be
taken out of the flask, washed carefully to remove all traces of agar, and then
potted up in a fine compost mix. For their first few weeks in the greenhouse they
need special care. Extra warmth and humidity, which can be provided in a small
propagating case, is often beneficial.

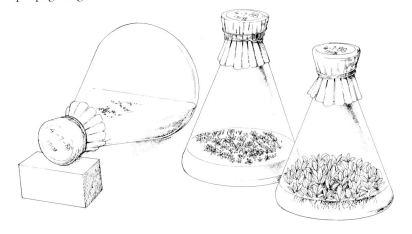

Orchid protocorms
and seedlings on
agar in flasks

Different kinds of orchids develop at different rates. Some of the quickest are the phalaenopsis species and hybrids, which can grow from seed to flowering size in as little as 18–20 months. Others take much longer. Four to six years is an average length of time for many different orchids.

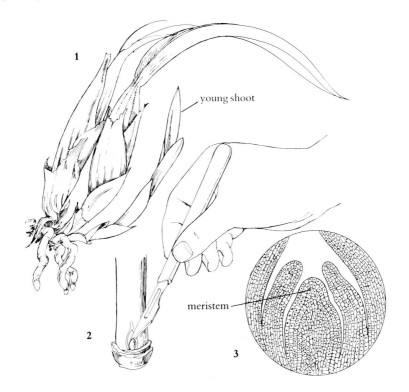

young shoot

meristem

1. Removal of young shoot, and 2. Dormant bud for meristem propagation; 3. Shoot tip in longitudinal section (greatly enlarged) with meristematic cells in centre

MERISTEM PROPAGATION

A feature of orchid culture, both commercially and as a hobby, is the high value placed on plants that have received awards from the Royal Horticultural Society (RHS), American Orchid Society (AOS) and other award-giving bodies around the world. Many people would like to have divisions of such desirable plants, and the demand makes their prices high. The advent of meristem propagation of orchids in 1960, by culturing and multiplying the apical meristem of a young shoot, and the various forms of tissue culture that have since been developed, have been extremely successful and have made it possible for many people to own and enjoy some of the best plants at the same price that they would have to pay for seedlings. The technique of growing new plants in this way is very similar to propagation from seeds, but because the starting material is already mature, the protocorms obtained by this method develop into new, flowering-size plants much more quickly. Sterile conditions, containers and plant material are used, and a warm growth chamber is necessary for the young plants on agar. After they are transferred to a normal orchid compost in the greenhouse they grow away very rapidly. This technique is not difficult, and modifications of it are carried out today in many parts of the world for a wide range of orchids.

6
Seasonal Care in the Greenhouse

There is always something to be done in the greenhouse by the owner of a collection of orchid plants; plants are best treated as individuals. They should be repotted after flowering or when the compost needs changing. Dead leaves and flowers should be removed continuously. They are unsightly in a well-kept greenhouse, as well as being a possible source of disease. A weekly or monthly check for pests and problems is highly desirable. Some chores and pleasures of the greenhouse are seasonal, however, and a brief summary of these may be useful.

SPRING

Early in spring it is useful to have a general inspection of every plant, its compost and container. This is the time to repot all those plants that have flowered during the winter months or have not yet reached flowering size. In northern temperate regions one should aim at completing all the repotting as early as possible, so that the plants can have all the advantages of a long growing season with the increased warmth and daylight of the summer months. This is also a good time for thorough cleaning of the benches and floor of the greenhouse.

Opposite: *Ada aurantiaca* from Colombia (see page 68)
Left: *Calanthe vestita* var. *rubromaculata* in Durban Botanic Garden (see page 75)

After repotting is the time when orchid plants need extra care and frequent misting over of the leaves. Keeping the new compost moist, but on the dry side, seems to encourage new roots to grow out in search of moisture and reduces the risk that old or damaged roots will rot; it must not be too dry or plants will become desiccated. The greenhouse glass will probably need a thick coating of 'Coolglass' or some other form of shading at this time.

Renanthera coccinea
(see page 109)

SUMMER

The summer and early autumn is the main growing period, when watering and feeding of the plants must be carried out more frequently. Care should be taken to respond to individual requirements. Some plants do well with more light and fertilizer during this period, whereas others grow best if they are moved to a more shady position during the brighter summer days. Ventilators and fans need to be checked every day. Most greenhouses will require extra shading above the glass. Some growers use one of the new thermal screen materials as an interior shade, which can be drawn across on sunny days but left open to ensure the maximum amount of light when it is cloudy. This is a good time to check the heating system and the exterior of the building, as repairs can be carried out more easily during the summer.

AUTUMN

When autumn comes the shading can be removed, and about a fortnight later any remaining paint should be cleaned off the glass to take advantage of all the light that is available during the winter. Fertilizer and water are gradually reduced, and the heating will be required on cool nights. From now on the heating will probably run almost continuously, keeping the temperature at the required minimum during the night and giving it a boost of at least 5°C (10°F) during the day.

WINTER

The winter months are the major flowering season, but there are quite a lot of species that regularly flower at other times. Many orchids have strong, erect flowering stems and do not require any staking, but others have slender or arching stems with many flowers, and look more pleasing if they are given some support. Upright canes or curved pieces of stiff wire are best. The ties should be as unobtrusive as possible, and should be put in place as the flower stems grow and before the buds open. The flowers will emerge and 'set' at a natural and attractive angle. With many orchids it is important to avoid changing the position of the plant on the bench, so that the flowers become evenly arranged on the spike and do not twist round to face the light.

Some growers use a thermal screen material, or polythene lining such as 'bubble glaze', as an aid to heat conservation during the winter. It is a good idea to clean the inside of the glass thoroughly before this is installed. The ventilators will be closed for most of the winter, but fans should be maintained and run continuously, despite their cooling effect, in order to keep the atmosphere buoyant.

Winter and early spring is the time to enjoy your plants in flower by bringing them into the house. It is also the time to learn more about them, by reading or by visiting orchid shows in various parts of the country.

It adds greatly to the interest of an orchid collection if all the plants are clearly and correctly labelled. Plastic labels and waterproof pens are generally used. Labels can be used to record a great deal of information in addition to the names of the plants. Many growers like to keep a catalogue of their plants, with a record of flowering time, country of origin, date of acquisition and repotting, and this can be brought up to date before the busy spring period comes round again.

Pleione humilis (see page 107)

7
Pests and Diseases

Orchids are not more prone to attack by pests and diseases than other greenhouse plants. Provided that their growing conditions are hygienic and buoyant, most plants will never need treatment with sprays or insecticides. But problems can occur, and it is as well to know which are the worst kinds of pests to look out for and how to deal with them.

A greenhouse should always be kept clean and tidy, with benches and pots free from weeds. Dead leaves and dying flowers should be removed regularly. New plants should be inspected most carefully before they are added to a collection. Whether they come from a garden centre, a well-known nursery or a friend, they may be harbouring pests, which should be destroyed rather than introduced to a new collection of plants. All insecticides and other chemicals should be used with the greatest care: gloves should be worn, and the manufacturer's instructions strictly followed. They must only be used in the correct concentration, and can be harmful to the plant if applied in bright sunlight or used when temperatures are high.

PESTS

Aphids are often a nuisance on young shoots and on flower buds, especially during the winter months. Unless they are very numerous they can usually be gently removed with finger and thumb, or killed off by spraying with soapy water. Malathion is the safest general-purpose insecticide for greenhouse use, and is effective against aphids and many kinds of scale insects.

Mealy bugs are more resistant because of their water-resistant outer covering. These sap-sucking insects lurk on the undersides of leaves, under the sheaths on pseudobulbs and stems, and within the bracts supporting the flowers. Regular inspection and treatment is the best means of keeping insect pests down to negligible proportions. Insecticides such as Malathion are best used as wettable powders rather than as liquids, which have xylene as a solvent. There is no danger of foliage burn with the wettable powders, though they may leave an unsightly deposit.

Insects that eat parts of orchid plants, especially the flowers, include **vine weevils** and **cockroaches**. Both are nocturnal, and the best way of dealing with them is to catch them in the act of feeding. Apart from catching pests, it can be a pleasure to be in a greenhouse in the evening – some orchids are powerfully scented then, and others have colours that glow under artificial light.

Caterpillars and other insect larvae can be voracious, causing devastation in just one night. Woodlice are sometimes a problem in bark composts, as they feed on decaying plant material and sometimes turn their attention to young roots. They are not easy to eradicate, but can be controlled by careful attention to good hygiene, regular cleaning of the greenhouse, and the use of a suitable powder sprinkled around the door and on the floor where they may enter.

Opposite:
Oncidium hybrid
(*O. sprucei* × *O. splendidum*) (see page 101)

59

Slugs and **snails** can do considerable damage to buds, flowers and young shoots. The best way to deal with them is to search for them at night with a torch and remove the marauders by hand. Several different kinds of bait are available, usually containing metaldehyde or methiocarb, and if used frequently these should help to keep the numbers down. Some growers swear that beer is the most successful kind of bait for slugs!

Mice are also heavy feeders on young buds and shoots if they intrude into a greenhouse.

Red spider mites and several species of false spider mites are probably the worst pests of orchid plants, and they are very difficult to eradicate. They are very small and hard to see, even with a magnifying lens, but the damage they do is readily recognizable. Small pits or tiny silver spots on the lower surface of the leaves are evidence of their presence. Other species make irregularly shaped depressions, often yellowish brown in colour, in the leaf surface. Mites multiply rapidly in favourable – warm and dry – conditions. This is usually the key to their control. If mites are present in a greenhouse, it means that the environment is not really quite humid enough for orchids. A heavy infestation of mites can be controlled with an acaricide such as Kelthane or Pentac. Both of these should be used in cool weather, and at least two applications should be made at ten-day intervals in order to ensure that the mites at all stages of their life cycle are killed.

FUNGUS AND BACTERIAL DISEASES

Black or brown spots on leaves and flowers, and watery patches in leaf tissue, are a sure sign that something has gone wrong and a pathogen has invaded the plant. Very often this is because of wrong or careless treatment of the plant. Overwatering, careless repotting, direct sunlight on a wet leaf, low temperatures, poor ventilation and stagnant air can all precipitate fungal or bacterial invasion. Usually the rot has gone too far for treatment by the time it becomes obvious. The best method of dealing with it is to remove the affected tissue and about 1 cm (0.5 in) of adjacent healthy tissue, and disinfect the cut surface with flowers of

Oncidium jonesianum (see page 101)

sulphur, Captan or Physan. Damaged parts should be removed and burned to avoid infecting other plants. Badly affected plants should be abandoned and burned for the sake of the rest of the collection.

VIRUS DISEASES

A number of different virus diseases have been identified in cultivated orchids. They are probably the worst of the problems, because at the moment there is no cure for them. The symptoms of virus infection are pale patches, often in the form of an irregular mosaic pattern, on the young shoots and leaves. These become brown or black as the plant ages. It is hardly worth keeping suspect plants, which often grow weakly and flower poorly, as they can be a source of infection to other plants through insect bites or cutting tools.

OTHER PROBLEMS

Discoloration of leaves can be caused by mineral deficiencies. They will disappear when the plants are given sufficient fertilizer. It is well worth giving suspect plants a teaspoon or two of Epsom salts (magnesium sulphate), sprinkled on the surface of the compost and watered in, once or twice a month.

Stunted growth may also indicate a lack of nutrients, particularly nitrogen. Lack of flowers, or fewer flowers than expected, can also be due to an unbalanced fertilizer programme, and may indicate a need for a higher concentration of potassium or phosphorus in the feeding programme.

Too much fertilizer, especially nitrogen, is likely to promote very long but weak growths and thin leaves; such plants will need extra staking or they may break. Too heavy feeding can also result in loss of leaves. Salts dissolved in the water supply, as well as chemical fertilizers or a build-up of excess salts in the potting medium, can cause leaf tip dieback. A generous flushing of the compost with plain water every month or so is very beneficial.

Distortions of the foliage sometimes occur on young growths, particularly in members of the *Oncidium* alliance, and also in cymbidiums and paphiopedilums. This usually occurs as a result of a severe check, such as dryness or low temperatures, during the early development of the shoot, and can be avoided by greater attention to these details for subsequent growths. It can also be a genetic defect; if a plant that regularly grows in an ugly way is too unsightly it should be abandoned.

8
Special Groups of Orchids

Orchids will grow and flower in a great variety of situations. Even without a heated greenhouse there are many different kinds that can be cultivated – in a garden, an alpine house or an unheated conservatory. All that is required is to choose carefully and to try to provide conditions as near as possible to those enjoyed in the wild by any particular species.

HARDY ORCHIDS FOR THE GARDEN

There are a number of very attractive terrestrial orchid genera from the northern temperate areas of the world that are completely deciduous during the cold weather. They do not begin their annual cycle of growth until temperatures begin to rise in spring; they flower during late spring or mid summer, set seed during the late summer and autumn, and die down again before the first frosts of winter.

Some of the species of the lady's slipper genus, *Cypripedium*, are completely hardy, and there are also a number of species of *Dactylorhiza* that make a

Opposite: *Cypripedium calceolus* on a calcareous hillside (see page 84)
Left: *Dactylorhiza foliosa* flowering well in a semi-shaded, moist position (see page 84)

Cymbidium eburneum (see page 82)

spectacular addition to the woodland border. Both genera require a humus-rich, moisture-retentive soil, which should neither become waterlogged nor be allowed to dry out completely. Any good garden loam can be made suitable by the incorporation of peat and decaying leaves into the top 30 cm (12 in) of soil. The dormant rhizomes or tuberous roots can be planted in this mixture. Dappled shade, or a position that is sunny for only part of the day, is suitable for several of the species. A few species prefer calcareous soils, including the European *Cypripedium calceolus*, and a suitable niche for this species can be prepared by adding small pieces of chalk or limestone to the prepared site.

Some of the grassland species, including the genera *Orchis* and *Ophrys*, grow well in lawns in various parts of the country. The only special care required is that they should not be mown early in the year, before or immediately after flowering. An area of unmown grass in a patch of lawn can look very attractive in an informal garden, especially when the orchids are accompanied by bugles, clovers, daisies and other low-growing plants. They should also be established while the tubers are dormant, and, because they come into growth rather earlier than the woodland species, it is probably best to introduce the tubers during the autumn. Each should be set in a small cavity lined with sharp sand, at least 5 cm (2 in) below the surface of the ground.

When purchasing terrestrial orchids it is important (for reasons of conservation) to ensure that they have originated as nursery propagated plants and have not been taken directly from the wild which is illegal.

ORCHIDS FOR A COLD FRAME OR ALPINE HOUSE

There are a number of orchids from the mountains of subtropical regions that either require frost-free conditions, or need a dry period during the cold weather, and are most easily accommodated in a cold frame or unheated greenhouse. They can be treated in the same way as many alpine plants. The most notable group are the species and hybrids of the genus *Pleione*, which originate from the highlands of Asia, ranging from the Himalayas across Burma, Thailand, China and into Taiwan. They grow best in shallow pans and need repotting annually into a fine, fast-draining but moisture-retentive compost. Repotting should be carried out in late winter, just as the new flowering shoots, which start the cycle of growth, begin to emerge. Some of the Japanese species of *Calanthe* and *Cypripedium* do well in pans in the alpine house or cold frame, and *Bletilla* is also very tolerant of this treatment.

PATIO PLANTS

Large stone or terracotta pots filled with some of the hardy and cool-growing orchids can make an attractive addition to groups of potted plants on a patio. Those that are dormant in winter, including *Bletilla* and the pleiones, need to be overwintered in a frost-free shed or garage, and then repotted as soon as they start growing in spring. During spells of mild weather they can be put outside, and once the risk of frost has passed they can be left there for the summer. A few of the larger cymbidiums that flower late in the season, like *C. lowianum*, look very attractive outside during a spell of mild spring weather. Some of the calanthes and cypripediums will enjoy cool conditions outside in a completely shady situation, and their large, soft leaves are very decorative. In a sunny position the different colour forms of *Epidendrum* Obrienianum are also attractive throughout the summer, though care must be taken when they are first put outside to move them gradually into the sunshine to avoid burning the leaves.

A to Z of Orchids

Angraecum leonis; a species collected by the author in the island of Grande Comore (see page 69)

In the notes on cultivation given in this section reference is made to the temperature conditions usually required by each orchid, as follows:

Cool: minimum night temperature of about 10°C (50°F)

Intermediate: minimum night temperature of 13°C (55°F)

Warm: minimum night temperature of at least 16°C (60°F) and preferably 18°C (65°F) or even more.

The usual flowering time of each species or hybrid in cultivation – spring, summer, autumn or winter – is given at the end of each description. The system for naming orchids is explained on pages 22 and 23.

ADA

A small genus with about eight species in western tropical America from Costa Rica south to Peru. Numerous leaves in two rows often hide the small pseudobulbs, and support several inflorescences in their axils. The flowers are showy, yellow, brown, greenish or orange-red, with similar sepals and petals and a broader lip. Several species have been used to make hybrid genera such as × *Miltadium* (Mtadm.: *Ada* × *Miltonia* × *Oncidium*); and × *Stewartara* (Stwt.: *Ada* × *Cochlioda* × *Odontoglossum*).

Several of the species grow at high altitudes in the wild, so need cool night temperatures in cultivation. They grow well in a bark-based compost. Cool.

A. aurantiaca (*A. lehmannii*, *Brassia cinnabarina*) The best-known species, with brilliant orange-red, long-lasting flowers during the winter months.

A. glumacea (*Brassia glumacea*, *B. imbricata*) The inflorescence has large papery bracts supporting the yellow-green flowers, which have chocolate markings and a white lip. Summer.

A. keiliana (*Brassia keiliana*, *B. cinnamomea*) Flowers similar to those of *Brassia*, but with the distinctive callus on the red-spotted, cream lip. Early summer.

AERANGIS

A small genus of epiphytic orchids from Africa and Madagascar. Most of the plants have a fan of dark green leaves and arching or pendent sprays of white flowers. They need a shady place in the greenhouse, where there is plenty of air movement so that their aerial roots dry out between waterings. Many grow best when securely tied to a slab of bark or mounted on a log, but some do well in pots or a basket in a bark-based compost. Cool or intermediate.

A. citrata (*Angraecum citratum*) A small species from the humid coastal forests of eastern Madagascar. It bears long sprays of palest yellow flowers. Spring.

A. confusa A medium sized species from the highlands of Kenya, with white flowers that are often tinged with pink or green. It is more frequently seen in cultivation than the widespread *A. brachycarpa*, whose flowers are similar but larger with longer spurs. Early summer.

A. ellisii Often misnamed *A. cryptodon*, which is rather different, this is the largest species in Madagascar, where it grows on trees or among rocks. The succulent leaves are widely spaced and the huge inflorescences bear graceful white flowers with long spurs. Autumn or winter.

A. mystacidii A widespread species, found from Malawi to the eastern Cape. Delightful flowers with curving spurs are produced in quantity on well-grown plants and are scented in the evening. Spring and autumn.

AERIDES

A genus of about 20 epiphytic species from southeast Asia, with elongated stems and flat, leathery leaves in two rows. The showy flowers are usually white or pink flushed with rose, amethyst or purple, and are borne in lax or dense pendent racemes. They are very fragrant.

These species require warm and humid conditions in the greenhouse, with moderately bright light and plenty of fresh air. They need water daily and dilute fertilizer frequently during the growing season, and should be kept on the dry side during the winter. They probably do best in hanging baskets, which give their long aerial roots plenty of space. A few intergeneric hybrids that bear spectacular flowers have been made with the related genera, for example × *Aeridovanda* (*Aerdv.*: *Aerides* × *Vanda*), × *Rhynchorides* (*Rhrds.*: *Aerides* × *Rhynchostylis*) and others. Warm.

A. multiflora (*A. affinis*) Flowers 2–3 cm ($\frac{3}{4}$–$1\frac{1}{4}$ in) across, similar to those of *A. rosea* but usually smaller and more widely spaced on a long raceme. Summer.

A. odorata Flowers 2.5–4 cm (1–$1\frac{1}{2}$ in) across, white, sometimes with a few purple spots and a green tip to the upturned spur. Summer. The best forms come from the Philippines and are sometimes distinguished as *A. lawrenceae*. Autumn.

A. rosea (*A. fieldingii*, *A. williamsii*) Flowers up to 3.5 cm ($1\frac{1}{4}$ in) across, rose or amethyst purple mottled with white and sometimes spotted, usually in a dense raceme. Summer.

ANGRAECUM

A genus of about 200 orchids in tropical and subtropical Africa, Madagascar and the adjacent islands. There is great variation in the size of both plants and flowers, which are greenish, white, yellow or ochre. They may be solitary or borne in long racemes. All the species grow and flower well in a greenhouse if conditions that suit their individual requirements can be provided. Intermediate or warm.

A. calceolus Small plants with bright green leaves, found on rocks and trees in Mozambique and all the islands of the western Indian Ocean. The green flowers are supported by green or brown bracts and are widely spaced on slender, upright racemes or panicles. Summer.

A. conchiferum Slender stems bear small leaves and attractive flowers with a large,

shell-shaped lip. This species comes from cool forests on the higher mountains between Kenya and the Cape. Spring.

A. distichum A small epiphytic species from West Africa and Uganda, with curious compressed leaves on slender branches. The small white flowers are borne singly in the axils of the glossy green leaves and flower synchronously, covering the plant with white stars. Summer or autumn.

A. eburneum One of the largest species and the first to be described from the island of Réunion. Different varieties are now known from Madagascar, the Comoro Islands and the eastern coast of Africa (*A. giryamae*). The rigid leaves are leathery, and borne in two rows along the stem. The apple green flowers have a conspicuous white lip on the upper side of the flower, with a long spur hanging down. Summer or autumn.

A. infundibulare A large but slender plant from the shady and very humid equatorial forests of Africa. The large, greenish white flowers have a broad lip with a funnel-shaped, curving spur. Summer or autumn.

A. leonis An attractive plant with curved, pointed, compressed leaves and pure white flowers. The best forms have been collected in the Comoro Islands; smaller ones are known in parts of Madagascar. Summer.

A. magdalenae A medium sized plant that grows among rocks in the highlands of Madagascar. The dark green leaves are erect on the fan-shaped plant, and the flowers are pure white.

A. sesquipedale The comet orchid is widely known for the long spur on its large, showy flowers. It is widespread along the eastern coast of Madagascar, and is also well known in cultivation, where it grows well in warm, humid conditions. Winter.

A. Veitchii (*A. eburneum* × *A. sesquipedale*) The first hybrid recorded, in 1899, between epiphytic orchids from Africa.

Ansellia africana
from East Africa

reaching nearly 1 m (3 ft) tall. The dense spike of vivid rose-purple flowers is borne in the axil of the leaf and may be 30 cm (1 ft) long. These orchids are widespread but not common in Mexico and Central America, and are easily grown in cultivation. They need a moisture-retaining compost with good drainage and plenty of light to flower well in spring or early summer. Cool.

A. alpinum Plants up to 30 cm (1 ft) tall with purplish pink flower spikes.

A. giganteum (*A. cardinale*) Handsome plants up to 1 m (3 ft) tall, larger than the closely related *A. spicatum*. The attractive pink-purple flowers are slightly smaller than those of *A. alpinum*.

Very floriferous, with long sprays of green and white flowers that are intermediate in size between those of the parents. Easy to grow. Winter.

ANSELLIA

The leopard orchids come from tropical and subtropical Africa. Their brown-spotted, yellow flowers appear during winter and spring from the apex of the tall canes or pseudobulbs, and occasionally also from leafless nodes near their base. The robust stems are 30 cm–2 m (1–6 ft) tall and bear many leaves in two rows. Old plants develop upright, pointed roots around the base, which may obscure the pot or basket in which they are growing. Intermediate to warm.

A. africana (*A. gigantea*, *A. nilotica*) Only one, rather variable species is now recognized in this genus. Plants require plenty of water and dilute fertilizer while new growths are developing and producing their leaves, followed by a cooler period, with less water and more light, in order to stimulate flowering. Winter and spring.

ARPOPHYLLUM

Brassavola digbyana
from Belize (see
page 73)

The hyacinth orchids are epiphytic or terrestrial plants, easily recognized by the single strap-shaped leaf arising from the top of the slender stem, and sometimes

× ASCOCENDA (*Ascda.*)

These hybrid orchids (*Ascocentrum* × *Vanda*) have become very popular with growers for their long-lasting flowers, which are produced throughout the year. Plants grow well in shallow pots or teak baskets in warm, humid conditions, and benefit from frequent feeding while in active growth. They are smaller plants than vandas and require less light to flower, but the flowers are almost as big as those of vandas, usually more numerous, and they have the bright, jewel colours of the ascocentrums. Warm.

Brassavola nodosa from Mexico (see page 73)

Recommended hybrids include Yip Sum Wah (orange-red), Medasand (red), Sunkist (yellow), Fiftieth State Beauty (pink) and Bangkok Beauty (blue).

ASCOCENTRUM

These small epiphytic orchids are much sought after for their brilliant flowers in shades of orange, rose red or vermilion. Plants are usually upright, with two rows of leaves and several racemes of flowers. They grow well in pots or baskets, supported with pieces of bark, and need good light and high humidity at all times. During the summer months they need water and dilute fertilizer daily except in dull weather. During the winter they should be kept drier and fed less frequently. Warm.

Four or five species occur in southeast Asia. Two have been widely used in intergeneric crosses with species and hybrids of *Vanda* to make × *Ascocenda*. Numerous other hybrids have been made with other vandaceous genera.

A. ampullaceum A small species with dark green, purple-spotted leaves and flowers a deep rose red. Early summer.

A. curvifolium A taller species with yellowish green, curved but narrow leaves. Flowers vermilion or scarlet with an orange and yellow lip and a purple column. Summer.

A. miniatum A small species with succulent or leathery leaves. Flowers golden yellow, orange or red. Summer.

BARKERIA

These are cool-growing orchids from Mexico and Central America, which differ from *Epidendrum* in their growth habit, flower structure and cultural requirements. They have rather few leaves on short, cane-like pseudobulbs surmounted by an erect inflorescence of few to many lilac, rose or magenta flowers, which are delicate but showy. The pseudobulbs lose their leaves during the winter, before or after flowering, and the plants need to be kept dry until new growth begins. They grow best when fixed to a bark slab or block of wood with plenty of space for the fleshy roots to attach themselves. Cool to intermediate.

B. cyclotella A beautiful species with deep magenta flowers in early spring.

B. elegans A handsome species whose flowers are rose pink, the lip white with a deep crimson blotch in front and a purple-spotted yellow column. This species is rare in cultivation. Winter.

B. skinneri One of the largest species, with 20–30 showy lilac, rose purple or magenta flowers on each raceme. The flowers last on the plant for three to four months during the winter.

B. spectabilis A summer-flowering species with large and attractive lilac flowers.

× BEALLARA (Bllra.)

This is a complex, multigeneric hybrid genus derived by several generations of breeding from representatives of four distinct natural genera, *Miltonia* × *Brassia* × *Odontoglossum* × *Cochlioda*. The genus was registered by the late W.W.G. Moir of Hawaii, and named in honour of the late J. Ferguson Beall of Vashon Island, Washington State, USA. Both these hybridizers have made great contributions to orchid-growing by their successful artificial hybridizing among the easily grown plants of the *Oncidium* alliance. Plants need intermediate or cool temperatures, high humidity, and water throughout the year.

× **Beallara Tahoma Glacier** The best-known grex resulting from the cross between × *Miltassia* Cartagena and × *Odontioda* Alaskan Sunset. It has large flowers of strikingly heavy substance, white or cream with dark red spots. Spring.

BLETILLA

Some of these nearly hardy orchids from Japan and China will survive in the garden except in severe winters, and make a colourful show in late spring. The corm-like pseudobulbs should be planted about 5 cm (2 in) deep in pots or in garden beds in a well-drained medium. No water should be given in spring until the shoots are about 10 cm (4 in) high or until the flower buds can be seen: premature watering encourages vegetative growth so quickly that flowers may abort. As soon as the leaves are fully expanded plants should be watered and fed frequently. When the leaves turn yellow and fall the plants become dormant and very little water is required. Cool or alpine.

B. striata (B. hyacinthina) The most common species, easy to obtain from garden centres and to grow. The flowers are borne in an upright raceme arising between the attractive pleated leaves. They are usually rose-purple, but white forms have recently become available. Early summer.

BRASSAVOLA

This genus contains about 15 species of epiphytic or lithophytic plants in tropical America, distributed between Mexico and Argentina. They all have slender or slightly thickened stems arising from a basal rhizome, each bearing a thickened leaf or, rarely, two leaves at its apex. The flowers are medium or large in size, with greenish white sepals and petals and a large white lip. They are scented in the evening.

Plants grow well mounted on bark slabs or blocks of wood, or potted in shallow pots or hanging baskets. They need plenty of light at all times. Cool or intermediate at night, with high daytime temperatures.

B. acaulis Plants from Central America, with rush-like leaves. The flowers have long, narrow sepals and petals and a pure white, heart-shaped lip. Autumn.

B. cucullata Plants from Central and northern South America. The flowers have long, greenish white sepals and petals, which are broad at the base. The lip is also long, acuminate and rounded at the base with fringed margins. Autumn.

B. digbyana (*Rhyncholaelia digbyana*) A spectacular species from Mexico and Belize. The stems are swollen to form a pseudobulb, and bear a broad, fleshy leaf. Flowers are pale green with a large fringed lip. Flowering time variable. This species has been used to make many beautiful crosses in the genera × *Brassocattleya* (*Bc.*) and × *Brassolaeliocattleya* (*Blc.*)

B. glauca (*Rhyncholaelia glauca*) A rare species from Mexico, Guatemala, Honduras and Belize. The whole plant is fleshy and glaucous green. Flowers pale green, white or pale lavender with a white lip. Spring.

B. nodosa (*B. venosa*) A species from very dry situations from Mexico to Panama and Venezuela, sometimes growing as an epiphyte on large cacti, often near the sea. Leaves fleshy and terete. Flowers showy, sepals and petals greenish, lip white with purple spots near the base. Autumn.

B. tuberculata (*B. fragrans, B. perrinii*) A robust species from Brazil and Bolivia. The flowers have yellow or greenish yellow sepals, spotted red; the petals are similar but lack spots, and have a white lip with a yellow blotch near the base. Summer.

BRASSIA

There are about 20 species of this genus in the tropical parts of the Americas, from Florida to Brazil. The plants are usually rather large epiphytes. A stout, creeping rhizome produces many roots and ovoid but compressed pseudobulbs surmounted by one to three leaves. The plants flower best if they are rarely disturbed. One or two long inflorescences arise from the base of each pseudobulb, bearing numerous showy, spidery flowers.

The plants grow well in pots or baskets in a bark-based compost that drains freely. They need humid but buoyant conditions. Watering and feeding with dilute fertilizer should be frequent during the summer months. During the winter plants need only sufficient water to prevent shrivelling of the pseudobulbs. Intermediate to warm.

B. caudata Flowers orange or yellow, marked with reddish brown; lip yellow or greenish with red-brown spots near the base. Summer.

B. longissima Large, orange-brown flowers with purplish maroon blotches; very elongated sepals. Summer.

B. maculata Flowers large, yellowish, spotted with reddish brown; lip rounded, white with reddish brown spots near the base. Early summer.

B. Rex This is a splendid hybrid with large flowers made from *B. verrucosa* × *B. gireoudiana*. Flowers large, pale green, with dark brown spots and greenish warts.

B. verrucosa Flowers pale green or cream, spotted with dark brown; lip covered with greenish warts in the lower half and red spots near the base. Spring and early summer.

× BRASSOCATTLEYA (Bc.) and × BRASSOLAELIOCATTLEYA (Blc.)

Some of the largest and brightest-flowered hybrids in the *Cattleya* alliance are actually intergeneric crosses of *Cattleya* or × *Laeliocattleya* with *Brassavola*, which are known as × *Brassocattleya* (*Bc.*) and × *Brassolaeliocattleya* (*Blc.*), respectively. They are easily grown under the same conditions as the parent genera. Intermediate.

Where *Brassavola digbyana* was involved in the breeding they have a very large lip with a frilled margin. Recommended hybrids are Norman's Bay and Bryce Canyon (rose magenta), Mount Hood (white or pale lavender), Malworth 'Orchidglade' and Fortune (yellow), Cadmium Light 'Sweet Lime' and Ports of Paradise (lime green). *Brassavola nodosa* has also been used as a parent; the progeny have small but brightly coloured flowers. Recommended examples are Binosa (lime green and purple), Ria Meyer (golden yellow) and Maikai (purple).

× *Brassolaeliocattleya* Norman's Bay 'Low's' (see page 73)

BULBOPHYLLUM

Plants in this huge genus are always recognizable by their swollen pseudobulbs bearing one or two leaves at the apex. In many of the 1000 or more species the flowers could be described as curious rather than beautiful, and each has an articulated lip which moves in the slightest breath of air. The genus is represented throughout the tropics, with the greatest numbers of species in the warmer parts of Asia and about 70 species in Africa.

In the wild most plants creep over the trunks or branches of trees or over rocks, with their pseudobulbs either arising close together from the basal rhizome or widely spaced. In cultivation they thrive best when mounted on slabs of bark or blocks of wood or are established in a shallow basket. Many grow well if moss can be encouraged to proliferate around their roots. They are easily propagated by division of the rhizome into pieces bearing not less than three pseudobulbs; smaller pieces take a very long time to become estab-

lished. Suitable night temperatures for the different species will depend on each one's provenance, species from the warmer climates at low altitudes requiring warmer conditions than montane ones.

B. barbigerum A dwarf plant from West Africa with small, flattened pseudobulbs. The long-lasting inflorescence bears maroon flowers that have a slender lip, its overall shape concealed by an abundance of long, whiskery hairs. Summer.

B. lobbii One of the best-known species from southeast Asia. It bears large, solitary flowers that are rather variable in colour, usually yellow or pinkish with red lines or spots. Summer.

B. macranthum An attractive species from Malaysia, Java, Sumatra and Borneo, with large, solitary, yellowish cream or rose purple, streaked or spotted flowers. The lateral sepals are sometimes partly united to form a hood over the small white lip, which is on the upper side of the flower. Early summer.

B. nutans The first species described in the genus, from Réunion. It has attractive groups of small, pinkish yellow flowers borne close together on a short nodding inflorescence. Summer.

B. purpureorachis This African species has the most conspicuous inflorescence. It can be as much as 60 cm (2 ft) long and 10 cm (4 in) wide, is spirally twisted throughout its length, and purplish brown and mottled. It bears small flowers in two rows along its midrib. Spring.

CALANTHE

The calanthes are nearly all terrestrial orchids, and more than a hundred species can be found in the tropics of the old world, mostly in Asia. There are two distinct groups: one has greyish pseudobulbs and deciduous leaves, the tall flower spikes appearing after the leaves have fallen; the other has small or inconspicuous pseudobulbs with persistent, large, plicate leaves that sometimes hide the flower spikes. The flowers are attractive, white, pink, yellow or lilac.

Plants grow best in plastic pots in a freely draining compost made up of peat, perlite and leafmould. Shady, humid conditions are required in summer, with a buoyant atmosphere and high daytime tempera-

tures. The deciduous types need to be allowed to dry out as the leaves turn yellow and fall, to induce flowering. Annual repotting in spring is beneficial for renewed growth and regular flowering.

DECIDUOUS SPECIES AND HYBRIDS

Well-grown specimens of the deciduous types produce very attractive flowers in large spikes. They are white, pink, red or combinations of these colours. They last a long time on the plant during the winter months and as cut flowers. Intermediate.

C. cardioglossa A pretty pink-and-white-flowered species from Thailand and neighbouring countries. The pink sepals and petals are reflexed. The white lip is heavily striped with purple and the spur white. Only two or three flowers are open at one time. Autumn.

C. rosea This species often has curiously constricted pseudobulbs. The flowers are a pretty shade of pink with a darker lip. Winter.

C. rubens Grows on limestone rocks in northern Thailand and Malaysia. The flowers are completely pink or white with a central red stripe on the lip.

C. vestita The most widespread species in the wild, occurring throughout southeast Asia from Burma to the Celebes. It is milky white in colour with a yellowish blotch on the lip and a greenish spur. Winter.

Calanthe Sedenii 'Harrisii' FCC/RHS (see page 76)

Catasetum saccatum from Brazil (see page 77)

Several distinct varieties have been described, including: var. *rubromaculata*, which has a reddish purple blotch on the lip; var. *regnieri*, which has a rose-coloured lip with a crimson purple blotch at its base; var. *williamsii*, with pale pink flowers often edged with a deeper pink and a dark crimson lip.

Hybrids There are also many beautiful hybrids in cultivation which have been derived by crossing the different species and varieties. Many of them are very robust with flower spikes 2 m (6 ft) long when they are well grown. Almost all are of great horticultural value. Recommended hybrids are Veitchii (pale pink), Sedenii and Bryan (pure white or almost so), William Murray (very like var. *rubromaculata*), Hexham Gem (rich deep pink), and Diana Broughton (crimson red).

EVERGREEN SPECIES AND HYBRIDS

This is the larger section of the genus, with tropical and temperate species. The former require water throughout the year and night temperatures of $12-15\,°C$ ($55-60\,°F$). The Chinese and Japanese species need a rest after the new shoots appear at the surface of the compost in autumn and can be hastened into growth by watering at the appropriate time in spring. Some of these are nearly hardy. Most of the species flower during late winter and spring.

C. discolor (*C. lurida*) A small species from the forest floor in Japan, almost hardy in sheltered places. The flowers are pale lilac or pink. Spring.

C. Dominyi It is worth noting this *Calanthe* hybrid (*C. masuca* × *C. furcata*), which was the first artificial orchid hybrid to flower. Seeds were obtained in England in 1854, and the first seedlings flowered in 1856.

C. striata (*C. sieboldii*) An elegant species from Japan, with dark green leaves and large yellow flowers. Early summer.

C. sylvatica (*C. masuca*, *C. natalensis*, *C. volkensii*) One of the first species introduced from India, and now recognized in the islands of the western Indian Ocean and Africa as well. The leaves are broad, and the flowers various shades of lilac, magenta and purple, sometimes with an orange callus on the lip. Summer.

C.triplicata (*C. furcata*, *C. veratrifolia*) A robust species with large leaves, widespread from India southeastwards to Australia. The large inflorescences bear pure white flowers, occasionally with a vermilion stripe along the centre of the lip. Summer.

CATASETUM

This genus is remarkable for the fact that two or three different kinds of flowers are borne, usually at different times, on the same plant: male flowers, female flowers, and in some species hermaphrodite ones also. The pollinia-bearing or male flowers appear most frequently, and are visited by large bees who are attracted to the musky odour they produce. A male bee enters the flower and scratches at the surface producing the smell. In doing so he touches an antenna, which releases the pollinarium in such a way that the viscidium becomes glued to his back. By the time the bee visits the quite differently shaped female flower on another plant, the pollinia are hanging below his abdomen in the right position to be deposited on the stigma.

All the species have stem-like, swollen pseudobulbs that bear large plicate leaves when they are young. They grow well in a variety of freely draining composts and require high temperatures during the summer months. During the early winter the leaves fall, leaving the basal sheath enfolding the pseudobulb and often a sharp spike where the midrib becomes detached. Many species flower throughout the summer, while others produce their blooms after the leaves have fallen.

About 50 species are now recognized from the tropical parts of Central and South America and the West Indies. A few spectacular hybrids have been registered recently, mostly made in Florida.

C. barbatum (*C. spinosum*, *C. crinitum*) A large epiphytic species from Guyana, Brazil and Peru. The male flowers are dark green with pinkish brown spots, the lip broad and concave with a bearded margin. The female flowers are smaller, fleshy and green. Summer.

C. pileatum (*C. bungerothii*) A large and distinctive species from Venezuela, Trinidad and Brazil. The male flowers have a broad white, golden or, rarely, red lip. The female flowers are smaller, green, the lip sometimes a rich golden yellow and forming a deep hood on the upper side of the flower. Autumn.

C. saccatum A species from Brazil and Guyana that has many distinct colour variants in the male flower, including orange, pinkish red, yellow, bright green and pure white. The three-lobed lip has a broad central spur and a fringed margin. The female flowers are yellowish green, with the lip forming a deep hood on the upper side of the flower. Summer.

C. tenebrosum A beautiful species from Peru and Ecuador. The male flowers have dark purplish brown sepals and petals and a lime green lip. The female flowers are hooded, greenish red. Summer.

Two closely related genera, *Clowesia* and *Dressleria*, are now separated from *Catasetum*, though they were often included in it in the past because they have a catapult mechanism for pollination. *Clowesia* has five species, distributed between Mexico and Venezuela. They all have a pendulous inflorescence of showy, pale green or pink flowers which are bisexual. *Dressleria* has one well-known species with white and orange, bisexual flowers on an erect raceme.

CATTLEYA

Some of the most flamboyant orchids belong in this genus, together with others that are very bright and colourful. In the wild they all grow as epiphytes or on rocks in tropical America. A number of upright pseudobulbs arise from a creeping rhizome. One to three leaves grow from the top of each pseudobulb, enclosing a sheath from which the inflorescence emerges. One to many showy flowers are borne on each growth, either as soon as it matures or after a wait of several months.

In cultivation the plants grow best in pots or baskets in a bark-based compost. They need a good balance between a prolonged dry resting period with a minimum temperature of about 10°C (50°F), and an active period in a moist, warm atmosphere with plenty of water and dilute fertilizer.

Many hybrids have been made and registered in the last hundred years and are more commonly grown today than the wild species. Several other genera, notably *Brassavola*, *Laelia* and *Sophronitis* have added their features of colour and shape to the flowers of these.

ONE-LEAVED SPECIES

C. dowiana A rare species from Costa Rica, Panama and Colombia. There are usually two, occasionally up to six golden flowers up to 15 cm (6 in) across, with a brilliant crimson-purple, velvety lip. Late summer.

C. labiata This was the first of the large flowered Brazilian species to be introduced to cultivation. The inflorescence bears two to five flowers, which are 12.5–15 cm (5–6 in) across with pale or deep rose sepals and petals and a rich magenta lip with a frilly border and a yellow blotch in the throat. There are several similar species from other areas in South America: *C. eldorado* (Brazil), *C. gaskelliana* (Venezuela), *C. mendelii* (Colombia), *C. mossiae* and *C. percivaliana* (Venezuela), *C. trianaei* (Colombia), *C. warneri* (Brazil), *C. warscewiczii* (Colombia), and others that are considered by some botanists as geographical variants of *C. labiata* while others prefer to regard them as distinct species. They differ in small respects, especially in the shape and coloration of the lip and their flowering habit, but each is rather variable. Nearly all have several different colour forms, including white ('Alba') forms, which have been introduced at various times and used in hybridizing. Spring, summer or autumn.

C. maxima A striking species from Ecuador, Colombia and Peru. The flowers are 10–12.5 cm (4–5 in) across, pale rose-lilac, the pale pink lip veined purple and with a central band of yellow. Winter.

C. rex A lovely species from Peru and Colombia, with flowers up to 15 cm (6 in) across. They are creamy white, the lip rose in front with yellow side lobes and the yellow throat veined red. Summer.

TWO- OR THREE-LEAVED SPECIES

C. amethystoglossa A vigorous species from Brazil. The tall stems bear three to twenty flowers that are 7.5–10 cm (3–4 in) across, sepals and petals white or pale pink spotted with dark purple, the lip deep rose magenta. Spring.

C. aurantiaca A fairly common epiphyte in Guatemala, Mexico, Honduras and El Salvador. The inflorescences usually have many flowers, 3–4 cm (c. 1½ in) in diameter, orange, yellow or orange-red, rarely white, the narrow lip marked with faint maroon stripes. Summer.

C. bicolor A pretty species from Brazil that is easily recognized by the absence of side lobes at the base of the lip. There are usually several flowers, up to 9 cm (3½ in) across; sepals and petals green, coppery brown or yellowish, the spade-shaped lip a brilliant pale purple. Late summer.

C. bowringiana A vigorous species from Guatemala and Belize, with glaucous green leaves and pseudobulbs. Many flowers up to 7 cm (3 in) across, usually a rich magenta colour. Pale forms that are almost blue, and much darker ones, are also known. Autumn. This species has been involved in the ancestry of several spectac-

Cattleya luteola from Brazil

ular hybrids, including *C.* Portia (*C. bowringiana* × *C. labiata*).

C. intermedia A pretty species from Brazil, often growing on trees or rocks near the sea. Flowers 10–12.5 cm (4–5 in) across, sepals and petals pale lilac or white, the mid lobe of the lip usually rich purple, but can be white or amethyst. Summer.

C. loddigesii A widely grown species from southern Brazil. Flowers 8–11 cm (3–4½ in) across, a pretty, pale rosy purple, with a white throat to the lip becoming yellow below. Summer.

C. luteola A small species from Brazil. Flowers 6–8 cm (2.3–3.3 in) across, yellowish green, the lip with faint crimson streaks. Summer.

C. nobilior A small, creeping epiphyte from Brazil. It has large flowers, 10–12 cm (4–5 in) across, pale rose-purple with a darker lip.

C. skinneri An uncommon species from Central America. Flowers 6–8 cm (2¼–3 in) across, vivid rosy purple with white in the throat of the lip. White forms with pale yellow at the base of the lip are also known, and others with a dark band in the throat. Early summer.

C. walkeriana This is similar to *C. nobilior*, but usually has a single leaf and smaller flowers. Its white form is particularly attractive and long-lasting. Spring.

Hybrids Many of the colourful hybrids in the *Cattleya* alliance are intergeneric hybrids, and some recommended plants are listed under × *Brassocattleya* (*Bc.*), × *Brassolaeliocattleya* (*Blc.*), × *Laeliocattleya* (*Lc.*), × *Sophrolaeliocattleya* (*Slc.*) and × *Potinara* (*Pot.*). There are also some beautiful white hybrids with very large, long-lasting flowers, often with a splash of yellow in the throat of the lip, that have been bred from some of the *Cattleya* species. Recommended white hybrids are Bow Bells, Bob Betts, Empress Bells, Karae Lyn Sugiyama, Swingtime, Henrietta Japhet, and Angelwalker.

Cattleya amethystoglossa from Brazil

CIRRHOPETALUM

A genus of 30 or more species and several attractive hybrids, unusual in the orchid family in having an umbellate inflorescence. The pink, cream, yellow or brownish flowers, often mottled or with various markings, are neatly arranged at the end of the rachis so that they radiate in a circle. They are mostly found in the warmer parts of Asia, though one species extends west to Africa and south to Australia.

Catasetum pileatum from Venezuela (see page 77)

Some authorities include these orchids in *Bulbophyllum*, but others keep them separate. Most of the species in cultivation are easily recognized by their lovely inflorescences and their flowers, which have greatly elongated lateral sepals. The rounded pseudobulbs grow from a creeping rhizome. Plants are most easily accommodated on bark or in baskets, and should be kept in shady but humid conditions. They need plenty of water throughout the year. Intermediate to warm.

C. graveolens (*C. robustum*) A large species from New Guinea and Indonesia with leathery leaves and succulent, green and gold flowers with a bright red or orange lip. Summer and autumn.

C. medusae An extraordinary species with many creamy flowers in a tight head. They are strongly scented and look very strange with their long, slender sepals. Summer.

C. ornatissimum Small plants with large flowers, from India. The sepals and petals are pale purplish brown, veined with dark purple and ornamented with purplish hairs around the margins. Autumn.

C. rothschildianum A handsome species, with few flowers in each inflorescence, but these are large, dark red and pink with broad sepals that have long tails. Summer.

C. umbellatum The only species in Africa and the islands of the western Indian Ocean. The flowers are pinkish or yellowish mottled with red, and appear at any time.

COCHLIODA

Six species are known so far in this genus of brightly coloured orchids. They are native to the highland forests of the Andes, and are apparently restricted to Peru, Ecuador and Bolivia. The plants are small and epiphytic, with short, flattened pseudobulbs bearing one to two leaves at the apex. The slender inflorescences arise from the base and bear numerous small to medium sized flowers in shades of white, pink, magenta, orange-red and scarlet. The petals are broader than the sepals, and the three-lobed lip has fleshy keels or crests on its surface.

These plants come from high altitudes and grow best in small pots or baskets with a freely draining compost enabling them to be watered frequently. They need cool nights throughout the year, and should be kept as cool as possible during hot summer weather, preferably under 25°C (75°F). Plenty of fresh air but high humidity throughout the year is also desirable. Cool.

Because of their bright colours several of the species have been used extensively in hybridizing with other members of the *Oncidium* alliance – see especially × *Odontioda* and × *Wilsonara*.

C. noezliana A species from Peru and Bolivia with orange-scarlet flowers. The callus on the lip is golden yellow and the column violet purple. Winter and spring.

C. rosea (*Odontoglossum roseum*) A species from Ecuador. The whole plant is dark green, tinged with violet. The flowers are produced in pendulous racemes and are rosy pink with a white column. Winter.

C. vulcanica This species from Peru and Ecuador has the largest flowers in the genus. They are a dark rose-pink or rose-purple colour on upright spikes. Late spring or autumn.

COELOGYNE

A large genus of more than a hundred species distributed throughout tropical Asia. They are found throughout a wide range of altitudes, usually growing on moss-covered rocks or trees. The pseudobulbs are variable in size and shape, with one or two leaves, close together or distant on a creeping rhizome. Some species flower from the mature pseudobulbs, others when the new growths first develop. Flowers are solitary or in long inflorescences, erect or pendulous, delicately hued but showy, in white, pink, ochre, yellow or green, often with bright yellow on the lip.

The species with pendent inflorescences look best if grown in baskets, but also do well, like the others, if grown in plastic pots. Species can be selected to suit the facilities available as they come from a wide range of climates. All species require a freely draining compost, good air movement, and plenty of water and dilute fertilizer during the growing season, followed by a period of less water when growth is complete.

COOL-GROWING SPECIES
(minimum 10°C (50°F))

C. corymbosa A highland species from the Himalayas. The erect inflorescences bear two to four white flowers, which have large yellow blotches outlined in red on the lip. Early summer.

C. cristata A widespread species in the wild, from Sikkim to Hongkong, and common in cultivation. The pendulous inflorescences are short with three to ten flowers, white with yellow ridges on the lip. Winter to spring.

C. dayana A widely cultivated species from the mountains of Malaysia, Sumatra and Java. When grown well it carries long, pendent inflorescences of cream and brown flowers. Spring and summer.

C. massangeana Similar to C. dayana, but the flowers arise from separate growths instead of the top of the leafy pseudobulb. Various flowering times.

C. mooreana A handsome species from Vietnam. The large, glistening white flowers have a little yellow at the base of the lip. Various flowering times.

C. nitida (C. ochracea) A common and widespread species from the northwest Himalayas eastwards to Thailand. Erect inflorescences with four to seven white flowers, yellow blotches on the side lobes of the lip, and a yellow centre bordered with red. Summer.

C. speciosa A larger species, from the highlands of Java and Sumatra. The drooping inflorescence bears one to three large flowers, which are greenish yellow, pale salmon or pure white. Summer.

WARM-GROWING SPECIES
(minimum 15°C (60°F))

C. asperata A lowland species from Malaysia, Sumatra and New Guinea. The pendent inflorescence has seven to ten large white flowers.

C. Burfordiensis A man-made hybrid between C. asperata and C. pandurata. A large plant, with robust inflorescences bearing attractive pale green and brown flowers. Early summer.

C. pandurata A large epiphytic species from Malaysia to Borneo. The handsome inflorescence carries several bright green flowers with blackish purple markings on the lip. Summer.

CUITLAUZINA

Formerly included under *Odontoglossum*, this Mexican genus has one species, which is easy to grow and a delight.

C. pendula (O. pendulum, O. citrosmum) Pendulous inflorescences up to 90 cm (3 ft) long bear between 20 and 30 pink and white flowers from the new growth. They are easily spotted with botrytis if plants are sprayed or watered carelessly. The plants are cool-growing and are best in pots or baskets suspended in the greenhouse where there is plenty of fresh air. They should be watered heavily during the growing season and allowed a complete rest during the winter. Spring or early summer.

CYMBIDIUM

The cymbidiums have become well known as flowering pot plants: colourful modern hybrids are available from many gardening outlets during the winter months. In the wild there are about 50 species, mainly epiphytes, distributed from India eastwards to Japan and south to Australia. They are robust plants with a large number of succulent roots and clumps of pseudobulbs enclosed by long, narrow leaves. Inflorescences arise from the base of the pseudobulbs, bearing large, showy flowers in a variety of colours.

The plants grow best in a freely draining compost based on medium-grade bark. Plastic pots are most convenient for them as they sometimes become very large and heavy. Cymbidiums grow well as houseplants provided they have enough light and fresh air. They can be put outside in a bright but sheltered place in summer when nights are frost-free. They need to be watered and fed frequently during summer, and given less water and fertilizer in winter. Cool.

SMALL SPECIES

C. devonianum An Indian species that has broad leaves and pendulous inflorescences. The greenish red flowers have a dark red, velvety lip. Spring.

C. eburneum An attractive species from India. The erect inflorescence bears one to three showy white flowers with golden ridges on the lip. Winter and early spring.

C. erythrostylum One of the most sought-after species, from Vietnam. The arching inflorescence bears four to seven white flowers with a deep red lip. Autumn to spring.

Cymbidium Burgundian 'Chateau' (see page 83)

Coelogyne mooreana from Vietnam (see page 81)

C. floribundum (*C. pumilum*) A delightful species from China and Japan, with erect, many flowered inflorescences. The sepals and petals are greenish yellow, often flushed with red, and the lip white with red markings. Spring.

C. goeringii (*C. virescens*) This Japanese species is hardy in sheltered gardens and can be grown as an alpine. The flowers are solitary on stout peduncles, usually green and white, but many colour forms are available in Japan.

C. tigrinum A pretty species from Burma with long-lasting flowers on an erect spike. The flowers are yellow-green with a white lip. Summer.

Small hybrids There are many good cultivars derived from breeding some of these smaller species with the standard types. Recommended crosses for home growing are Showgirl, Strathdon (white-pink); Ivy Fung, Mimi, Strathann, Miniature's Delight (red); Putana, Starbright, Leodogran (pink); Dag, King Arthur, Sara Jean, Tommy (green); Sylvia Miller (yellow).

LARGE SPECIES

C. hookerianum (*C. grandiflorum*) A species from India with tough, leathery leaves. The arching inflorescences bear large lime green flowers with a red-spotted white lip. Winter and spring.

C. insigne This species from Thailand is medium in growth habit but has rather tall, erect inflorescences. The flowers are variable in shades of white and pink with golden ridges on the lip. Early spring.

C. lowianum A very distinctive species from India, Burma and Thailand. It has arching sprays of many green and gold flowers each with a red, V-shaped blotch on the lip. Early spring.

C. tracyanum A scented species that flowers in autumn or early winter. The curved sprays bear many flowers, which are greenish yellow, heavily striped with brown, the lip pale yellow with red or brownish purple spots. Autumn.

Hybrids of standard cymbidiums Hybrids derived from many generations of artificial hybridizing among these larger species and their progeny are more widely cultivated than the original species. They

are large plants requiring a lot of space for their long leaves, but the inflorescences last up to two months in perfection. Many have become widely available as a result of meristem propagations, and some of the best clones are easily obtained. A small selection of good clones can give much pleasure during the winter months. Recommended hybrids include Angelica 'Advent' and 'December Gold' (early flowering yellows), Cariga 'Tetra Canary' (yellow with red banded lip), Spring Glory 'Dual Gold' (yellow/orange with dark crimson lip), Miretta 'Cherub', Sparkle and Fort George 'Lewes' (green), Highland Surprise, Del Rosa 'The King' and Howick (white), Kurun, Western Rose, Vieux Rose and Barlow Rose (pink), Sensation, Hamsey 'The Globe' and Ngaire (red), Burgundian 'Chateau' and Rothesay 'Black Label' (brown).

Hybrids between the two groups The most recent development among cymbidiums is the combination of these two distinct groups of hybrids, so it is now possible to obtain relatively small plants with large flowers that make very attractive pot plants. Recommended hybrids are Aviemore and Castle of Mey (shades of pink), Strathbraan (a range of colours including green, pink and cream), Grouville Bay (green) and Volcanic Flash (red).

Miniature
Cymbidium
Tommy

Cypripedium reginae
from North
America (see page
84)

CYPRIPEDIUM

The lady's slipper orchids are widespread terrestrial orchids in the Northern Hemisphere. Most species occur in Asia and in North America, two in Mexico and one in Europe.

Several of the species can be grown in gardens in semi-shaded woodland conditions. They also do very well in pots in a cool greenhouse or conservatory where alpines are grown. The best compost is a mix containing peat, loam and sand, sometimes with sphagnum moss added. The plants need moist but airy conditions while in full growth during the spring and summer, but should be kept cool and drier while dormant. The new growths appear as tight buds in early winter, after the foliage has died down, but they remain dormant for several months and only start to grow in mid-spring, one to two months before flowering. Rhizomes can be purchased from bulb suppliers while they are dormant, but they are often incorrectly named.

Each stem bears one or several plicate leaves and is topped by one to several attractive flowers in a variety of colours. The slipper-shaped lip is their most distinctive feature, and it often provides a colourful contrast with the rest of the flower. Cool, alpine or garden.

C. acaule The moccasin orchid is a North American species from the edges of woodland, where it grows in freely draining soil. The sepals and petals are brownish but the large lip is deep pink. Early summer.

C. calceolus Different varieties of this species occur in North America and Europe. The sepals and petals are dark brown or dull green, sometimes twisted, and the bulbous lip is bright yellow. Plants usually grow in a partially shaded situation and flower in early summer.

C. debile An interesting species, with a pair of leaves between which the small, nodding, green flower emerges. Summer.

C. formosanum Each has an opposite pair of rounded, plicate leaves and a white, greenish or pale pink flower with darker pink spots. Summer. *C. japonicum* is rather similar.

C. reginae This is the most showy species and is the queen lady's slipper of North America. It bears several flowers on each stem. They are white or pale pink with a deeper pink lip. It grows naturally at the edge of wet bogs and needs a moist compost. Summer.

DACTYLORHIZA

The marsh orchids are good plants for a woodland or partly shaded border in temperate gardens. Their common name indicates the damp habitat that some of the species favour, but others are grassland or heath plants. All grow well as alpines in an open, well-structured compost that drains freely, and flower in mid-summer. After flowering they should be allowed to dry off gradually and spend the winter in the dormant state. Repotting of the hand-shaped tubers is desirable in spring. Clumps in the garden can be lifted and divided at this time. Alpine or garden.

D. elata A tall species with plain green leaves from southwest Europe. The heads of magenta flowers are 10–30 cm (4–12 in) long.

D. foliosa A rare species in Madeira, and much sought after in cultivation elsewhere. The leaves are light green, and many magenta flowers are borne in spikes 5–15 cm (2–6 in) long. The flowers are broader than those of *D. elata*.

D. × grandis A natural hybrid of the common spotted orchid (*D. maculata*) and the southern marsh orchid (*D. praetermissa*) that is widespread in England and Europe and sometimes seen in gardens. A vigorous plant with spotted leaves. Flowers deep pinkish purple in heads up to 20 cm (8 in) long.

DENDROBIUM

This is one of the largest of the orchid genera, with more than 900 species distributed throughout Asia, from India to Japan and south to Australia and New Zealand. The plants are epiphytic or lithophytic with swollen, usually cane-like, stems or pseudobulbs. The inflorescences are lateral, usually near the top of the stems, mostly with rather large, showy flowers.

Because of their wide range of habitats over a large part of the globe, dendrobiums exhibit a wide range of growing requirements. They nearly all do best in rather small pots or slatted baskets with a freely draining compost. Some grow best when mounted on slabs of cork oak bark. All plants require good light, and plenty of water and fertilizer while growing. Many need a cool, dry rest once growth is complete for the season.

COOL-GROWING SPECIES

Many of the Indian and Australian species do best with short, warm or hot growing seasons followed by a cool dry winter. They flower in spring from buds that develop tantalizingly slowly during the winter months. Cool.

D. aphyllum (*D. pierardii*) Slender pendent stems bear two to three flowers at every node, delicate pale pink and yellow. *D. primulinum* is similar but has shorter stems and larger flowers.

D. chrysotoxum Slender, erect pseudobulbs, which are swollen in the upper half and leafy at the top. The golden yellow and orange flowers are borne in huge pendent clusters, like bunches of grapes, but only last one week.

D. densiflorum Very similar to *D. chrysotoxum*, but with larger plants and bigger flower clusters.

D. farmeri Similar to *D. chrysotoxum* but smaller, the flowers pale pink with an orange lip.

D. fimbriatum Long slender canes, upright or pendent, with golden yellow flowers. The var. *oculatum* has a maroon patch on the lip and is the form that is grown most often.

D. formosum The paperwhite dendrobiums are easily recognized by the black hairs clothing their stems. Their large, papery white flowers with a splash of yellow in the throat are distinctive and long-lasting. The beautiful hybrid × Hawaian King is derived from a cross with another of the paperwhite dendrobiums, *D. infundibulum*, by several generations of breeding.

D. kingianum Small plants from Australia with pretty pink flowers in a range of shades. Winter.

D. lindleyi (*D. aggregatum*) This has short flattened pseudobulbs each with a single leaf and a pretty inflorescence of golden flowers.

D. moschatum Long slender canes with apricot flowers and a slipper-shaped lip. The flowers are scented but short-lived.

D. nobile The best-known species from India, with rose and white flowers and a maroon blotch in the lip. Many colourful hybrids have been bred from it by Dr Jiro Yamamoto, and are popular in cultivation. Recommended hybrids are Yukidaruma 'The King' (snowy white flowers with a maroon throat), Golden Blossom (many different clones are available in various shades of yellow), Utopia 'Messenger' (dark reddish purple), Christmas Chime 'Asuka' (milky white flowers with purple tips).

D. speciosum A robust lithophytic species from Australia, with huge sprays of short-lived cream flowers. Winter.

D. thyrsiflorum Similer to *D. densiflorum*, but with cream and orange flowers in huge bunches.

D. williamsonii The black haired stems bear ivory white or yellowish flowers with a bright red blotch on the lip. Winter and spring.

COOL-GROWING SPECIES, NO DRY PERIOD

Many of the species from higher altitudes grow best if they are kept moist at the roots throughout the year. The atmosphere should always be buoyant around the

Dendrobium Penang Candy

plants. There are a number of species from New Guinea that are very attractive, including *D. cuthbertsonii* (*D. sophronites*), which has solitary flowers that are bright red, pink, magenta, orange or yellow; *D. lawesii* has red, tubular flowers; *D. vexillarium* has a tufted growth habit with yellowish green flowers; *D. violaceum* is usually pink; and *D. victoriareginae* is an unusual shade of pale bluish violet.

WARM-GROWING SPECIES

The species from tropical areas and the hybrids derived from them should not be allowed to stay dry for long periods. They need a higher minimum temperature during winter nights and as much warmth as possible during the day. Intermediate to warm.

D. anosmum (*D. superbum*) Long slender canes, usually pendulous, to 2 m (6 ft) long. Flowers large and showy, pink-purple with deep purple in the throat. Late winter to spring.

D. bigibbum Upright canes bearing erect inflorescences of up to 20 lilac or purple flowers. Large-flowered plants are sometimes distinguished as *D. phalaenopsis* which is widely used in hybridizing to make the very popular Pompadour-type dendrobiums, which last up to six weeks as cut flowers. Recommended hybrids are

Encyclia vitellina from Mexico (see page 89)

American Beauty, Garnet Beauty, Hickem Deb, Mauai Beauty, Penang Candy and many others. Spring.

D. lasianthera Very large plants with erect stems up to 2 m (6 ft) tall. Long inflorescences with many flowers of dark crimson red, petals twisted. Summer.

DENDROCHILUM

The necklace orchids have very elegant inflorescences of many tiny flowers. There are over 120 species in southeast Asia, the Philippines and New Guinea. The plants have slender, one-leaved pseudobulbs that grow close together in tufts. The inflorescences are produced on the new growths before the leaves mature. After flowering the plants need plenty of water and fertilizer until the pseudobulbs are fully grown and the leaves have expanded fully. Shallow pots or pans of well-drained compost are best. Intermediate or warm.

D. cobbianum (*Platyclinis cobbiana*) Inflorescences up to 50 cm (20 in) long. Flowers creamy white with a golden lip. Autumn.

D. filiforme (*Platyclinis filiformis*) A very delicate orchid with 100 or more tiny

Dendrobium lindleyi from India (see page 85)

golden flowers on each fine inflorescence, 30–40 cm (12–16 in) long. Summer.

D. glumaceum Easily recognizable by the large straw-coloured bracts that support the white, scented flowers. Inflorescences erect or drooping, 15–30 cm (6–12 in) long. Winter or early spring.

DIAPHANANTHE

The diaphanous flowers of this pretty African genus give it its name. Nearly 50 species have been described. They all have green, yellow, ochre or whitish flowers borne between two rows of leaves on short or long-stemmed plants. They look best established on pieces of bark or in hanging baskets, and need humid, shady conditions throughout the year. Most plants need to dry out completely between waterings. Intermediate.

D. bidens A long-stemmed species with 10 cm (4 in) sprays of salmon pink flowers. Summer.

D. fragrantissima A short-stemmed species with thickened, succulent leaves. The inflorescences of cream or yellowish flowers are 15–25 cm (6–10 in) long. Summer.

D. kamerunensis Short-stemmed plants with broad leaves and few, large green flowers on each inflorescence. Summer.

D. pellucida A large-leaved plant with inflorescences up to 60 cm (2 ft) long. Lovely translucent cream or pale yellow flowers with a fringed margin. Winter.

D. rutila A long-stemmed plant that is usually tinged reddish purple. The pale green flowers are yellowish or reddish on sprays up to 15 cm (6 in) long. Autumn to winter.

DISA

The 'Pride of Table Mountain' from the Cape Province of South Africa is the best-known orchid in this genus. More than 120 species are known throughout Africa, and several from Madagascar. Only a few South African species are in cultivation, but many hybrids of the larger flowered species have become popular in recent years. The stems arise from a basal rosette of leaves and are sheathed with short, pointed leaves along their length. They bear one to several striking flowers during the summer months. The sepals are large, the dorsal one hooded and spurred, the petals and lip very small.

They are all terrestrial plants requiring a moist, peaty, but well-drained compost and a buoyant atmosphere at all times. Cool.

D. racemosa A tall species with many cerise-coloured flowers.

D. tripetaloides The easiest to grow. A small species with small, spotted, white or pale pink flowers that are produced in succession over a long period. A bright yellow form is rare.

D. uniflora (*D. grandiflora*) The best-known species, with striking orange-red or pinkish red flowers.

Recommended hybrids derived from these three species include Diores, Foam, Kewensis, Kirstenbosch Pride and Veitchii.

DORITIS

This small genus of two or three species differs from *Phalaenopsis*, which it resembles and breeds with, by the conical mentum at the base of the lip. The flowers are showy, on tall inflorescences. The plants are monopodial, with leaves in two rows. They are found in Asia from Sri Lanka to Sumatra.

Plants grow well and form large clumps in pots or baskets in a bark-based compost. They need water and fertilizer when they are in active growth, often throughout the year. Intermediate to warm.

D. pulcherrima (*D. esmeralda*, *D. buyssoniana*) A terrestrial plant in Burma, Malaya and Sumatra. Flowers usually deep mauve purple, but paler forms, as well as bluish and white ones, are known. Summer.

This orchid is best known as a parent or ancestor of the colourful hybrids × *Doritaenopsis* (*Dtps.*) (*Doritis* × *Phalaenopsis* species and hybrids), to which it bequeathes upright stems of glowing, long-lasting flowers. Recommended hybrids are Coral Gleam, George Moler, Lady Jewel, Memoria Clarence Schubert, Pretty Nice and Red Coral.

DRACULA

A picturesque genus of orchids whose 60 species have sometimes been included in *Masdevallia*. Small to medium sized plants with a creeping rhizome bear slender one-leaved stems. The inflorescences are pendulous, and the colourful flowers are well displayed when the plants are grown in baskets. The flowers have large, spreading sepals, small petals and a hinged lip.

All the species come from high altitudes in the American tropics. In cultivation they require moist, shady conditions and a water supply throughout the year. Cool.

D. bella An attractive species from Colombia. Flowers large and showy. Sepals yellow or cream, densely mottled with maroon or crimson. The lip is white and shiny. Autumn.

D. chimaera (*Masdevallia chimaera*, *M. roezlii*, *M. wallisii*) A curious species from Colombia. Flowers on erect stems, large and striking. Sepals ochre-yellow, heavily mottled with purplish red, drawn out into long tails at their tips and with the whole inner surface covered with hairs. The lip is pale mauve, shell-shaped. Winter.

D. vampira The largest and most sinister-looking of the species, from Ecuador. The flowers are very dark, almost black, and short-lived. Spring.

DRYADELLA

Another group of epiphytic orchids that have recently been separated from *Masdevallia*. They have narrow, fleshy leaves and dainty flowers in rather dull colours, greenish yellow or brownish, spotted with red or purple, often on rather short stems. The almost open buds resemble a bird's head in shape, which has given this group the nickname 'partridge in the grass'. The plants are small, neat and easy to grow in a well-drained compost in small pots or mounted on tree fern fibre. They require moist, airy conditions and water throughout the year. Cool.

D. edwallii Flowers on short stems, greeny yellow with dull red spots and a red lip. Summer.

D. lilliputana Flowers on long stems above the leaves, cream spotted red with a yellowish lip. Winter.

D. zebrina Flowers green spotted with crimson, the lip deep red but somewhat hidden by the dorsal sepal, which curves over in front of the flower. Spring.

ENCYCLIA

Approximately 150 species of *Encyclia* are known from the Caribbean region, Central America and tropical South America. Their stems form rounded or pear-shaped pseudobulbs clustered together, each with one or more stiff and leathery leaves. The inflorescence arises between the leaves and is often branched with many small or medium sized showy flowers.

The plants are mostly epiphytic or lithophytic, and in cultivation do best in shallow pots or mounted on bark slabs. Most species require warm daytime temperatures. Intermediate.

E. aromatica A varied species with cream, green, yellow or brownish flowers. Spring.

E. chacaoensis This is one of the cockleshell orchids, with a typical rounded lip that is often striped with red or violet on the upper side of the flower. The rest of the flower is cream or pale green. *E. chondylobulbon*, *E. cochleata*, *E. fragrans* and *E. radiata* are similar. Summer.

E. citrina A pendent epiphytic species with glaucous leaves and pseudobulbs. Flowers large and waxy, bright yellow and scented. Spring and summer.

E. cordigera Upright with large flowers. Sepals and petals purplish brown, the lip bright rose-pink or white. Early summer.

E. mariae Lime green flowers with a large white lip. Spring.

E. vitellina A greyish green plant with upright sprays of brilliant orange-red flowers. Winter.

EPIDENDRUM

Many hundreds of orchids are accommodated in this large genus, some brilliantly coloured but others rather dingy. There are epiphytes and terrestrials in many tropical parts of the New World, many with slender, reed-like stems bearing leaves in two rows and a terminal inflorescence. They grow well in pots in a freely draining compost. Some of the creeping species do better mounted on a slab of bark. Cool to intermediate.

E. cinnabarinum A tall species from Brazil and Venezuela, with large heads of brilliant orange-red flowers. Summer.

E. difforme A small epiphyte with lime green flowers, from Florida southwards. Various.

E. falcatum Pendulous epiphytes from Mexico with a creeping stem, swollen succulent leaves and large greenish yellow and white flowers. Winter. *E. parkinsonianum* is very similar.

E. ibaguense (*E. radicans*) Plants of this orchid, and the similar *E. Obrienianum* (*E. evectum* × *E. radicans*) are sometimes known as the poor man's orchids because they grow so easily all over the tropics, almost as roadside weeds in many places. Creeping or scandent plants. Flowers orange or rose-red. Almost all year round.

E. ilense A rare species from Ecuador with a large, fringed white lip saved from extinction in a tiny habitat by propagation in cultivation. Winter.

E. nocturnum A tall species with broad leaves and a few large white flowers. Spring.

E. paniculatum Very varied plants, often up to 2.5 m (8 ft) tall. Flowers small, in large drooping clusters, lime green and white. Autumn.

E. pseudepidendrum A Costa Rican species with brilliant, waxy, lime green and orange flowers. Winter.

Several hybrids have been made with species and hybrids of other genera in the *Cattleya* alliance. Two well-known hybrids are × *Epicattleya* Fireball (*C.* Lutata × *E. cinnabarinum*), which is a tall, reed-stemmed plant with red flowers; and × *Epiphronitis* Veitchii (*E. radicans* × *Sophronitis grandiflora*), which has small plants with rich red flowers.

Euanthe sanderiana var. *alba* from the Philippines

EPIPACTIS

The helleborines are mostly woodland plants in the wild, and are spread throughout the northern temperate region. Only a few have been tried in gardens but at least two do well at Kew, one at the base of a rock wall (*E. gigantea*) and one in a sheltered woodland garden (*E. palustris*).

Epidendrum pseudepidendrum from Costa Rica

E. gigantea This North American species grows well and multiplies quickly where it

has good drainage and is undisturbed. There are up to 15 flowers on erect stems to 60 cm (2 ft) tall. They are mostly greenish brown with pink petals and lip. Plants have recently become available in quantity as the species has been successfully propagated by tissue culture techniques.

E. palustris The European marsh helleborine is usually taller than the preceding species, 30–90 cm (1–3 ft) tall, and grows in wet places, preferably on calcareous soils. The flowers appear in summer, and are greenish yellow with a conspicuous white lip.

ERIA

Many of the plants and flowers of this genus of more than 500 species of Asiatic orchids are rather insignificant, but a few are attractive and common in cultivation. The stems are pseudobulbous, creeping or cane-like, and the leaves very varied, some of them hairy. Spikes and flowers are sometimes hairy too and may have conspicuous bracts. The flowers are usually small, white, pink or greenish with yellow or red markings. Cool to intermediate.

E. coronaria (*E. suavis*) Medium-sized plants. Flowers white or yellowish with several dark red markings along the lip. Winter.

E. spicata (*E. convallarioides*) The lily of the valley orchid has dense spikes of small, white, bell-shaped flowers. Summer.

EUANTHE

One of the most beautiful vandas from the Philippines is often accepted by botanists as the only member of the genus *Euanthe*. Its lip structure is rather different from that of other species of *Vanda*. In cultivation the plants need good light and high humidity. During the summer they need plenty of water and dilute fertilizer, and some shade on the brightest days. Pots or baskets containing a bark-based compost are suitable containers. Warm.

E. sanderiana (*Esmeralda sanderiana*, *Vanda sanderiana*) Plants are large and upright, with two rows of narrow leaves. The flowers are in large axillary racemes, flat and attractive, pale or deep pink suffused with brown markings in the lower half. A white and green variety has been described as var. *alba*. Various.

EULOPHIA

There are over 200 species of this terrestrial orchid genus throughout the tropics, but the majority occur in Africa. The underground stems consist of chains of irregularly shaped pseudobulbs, from which annual growths of leaves and flower spikes emerge. A few species, however, have upright pseudobulbs above ground that bear deciduous leaves. These species have proved amenable to cultivation and are treasured for their long-lasting flower spikes. A well-drained compost and a period without water corresponding to a natural dry season are beneficial for these. Intermediate.

E. guineensis A tropical African species with broad leaves and an attractive upright spike of showy flowers. The narrow sepals and petals are pale purplish green, and the large lip is pink, rose or purple with darker veins. Summer.

E. streptopetala (*E. krebsii*, *E. paivaeana*) A species from southern and eastern Africa

Habenaria radiata from Japan (see page 92)

with broad, plicate leaves. The tall spikes are long-lasting, with brown and yellow flowers produced successively. Summer.

HABENARIA

The rein orchids are remarkably numerous terrestrial orchids throughout the tropics, but they are rarely seen in cultivation. Many grow from underground tubers in grasslands or boggy areas with acid soil. The flowers vary in size and colour but are mostly green, yellowish or white. They all have a conspicuous lip, which is spurred at the base.

A well-drained peat and grit compost is suitable for most species. After flowering it is important to continue feeding and watering the plants until the stems are quite brown, as next year's tuber is developing at this stage. A dormant period of several months is usually necessary before the new shoots appear, when watering can begin again.

H. radiata (*Pecteilis radiata*) A species from Japan and Korea. The scented white flowers have a large, fringed lip. Best grown as an alpine in pots that are allowed to dry out in winter. Late summer.

H. rhodocheila (*H. militaris*) A tropical orchid that is widespread in southeast Asia. The seasonal rosettes of leaves are attractively spotted, and the greenish flowers have a large, four-lobed, orange or scarlet lip. Very showy and easy to grow in a well-drained compost. Intermediate. Autumn.

LAELIA

A lovely genus of about 75 species in tropical America, with most species in either Mexico or Brazil, epiphytic, lithophytic or terrestrial. They all have thickened pseudobulbs that bear one or two leaves, arising from a basal rhizome. The pretty flowers are borne on long peduncles from the apex of each pseudobulb in shades of pink, lilac, purple, red, orange, yellow or white.

Plants grow well in shallow pots, slatted baskets, or mounted on slabs of tree fern fibre or cork oak bark. Bright light and good ventilation are essential at all times.

BRAZILIAN SPECIES

The Brazilian species and the hybrids derived from them require intermediate temperatures.

L. cinnabarina Lithophytic, stems 12–25 cm (5–10 in) long. Flowers ten to fifteen, bright cinnabar red. The epiphytic *L. harpophylla* has similar flowers on shorter inflorescences, and very slender stems. Spring.

L. crispa Epiphytic, stems 15–30 cm (6–12 in) tall. Flowers four to nine, white with a purple lip. *L. lobata* is of similar appearance. Summer.

L. crispata (*L. rupestris*) Lithophytic, stems 4–10 cm (2–4 in) long. Flowers two to ten, pale pink with a purplish lip. *L. longipes* and *L. mantiqueirae* are similar. Spring.

L. flava Lithophytic, with short stems, 4–20 cm (2–8 in) long and with tall flower spikes. Medium sized flowers, four to ten, bright canary yellow. Several other yellow-flowered laelias that grow on rocks have been described recently, including *L. bradei*, *L. briegeri*, *L. mixta* and *L. macrobulbosa*. Late spring.

L. perrinii Epiphytic, with stems 15–25 cm (6–10 in) long. Flowers two to three, large, flat and well-displayed, rose-pink with rich magenta lip. Early winter.

L. pumila Epiphytic, a dwarf species with stems up to 7 cm (3 in) high. Large, flat flowers with broad petals, pale rose-purple with a much darker lip. Spring or autumn.

L. purpurata The 'king of the orchids' is epiphytic, stems up to 50 cm (20 in) long. Flowers two to nine, large and showy, white or delicate pink with a rich purple lip. Forms with white, rose, carmine or purple lips are also cultivated. Summer.

L. tenebrosa Epiphytic, stems up to 30 cm (12 in) long. Flowers large, three to eight, coppery brown with a dusky purple lip. Summer.

L. xanthina Epiphytic, stems slender, 15–25 cm (6–10 in) tall. Flowers two to five, clear yellow, white on the lip with crimson markings. Much larger than *L. flava*. Spring and early summer.

MEXICAN SPECIES

Many of the Mexican species come from high altitudes, where they grow on rocks and trees in open situations and are in the clouds in the hottest part of the year. There is a pronounced dry season of several months' duration, when many species flower on long slender stems. In cultivation the plants need to be shaded but warm during the summer, and much cooler with bright light and little if any water during the winter. Cool.

L. albida Short, ovoid pseudobulbs with two leaves. Flowers five to nine, white, pink or rose. Winter.

L. anceps Short, four-angled pseudobulbs with one or two leaves. Flowers two to five, varied, deep rose pink with a darker lip but white and pale forms are also known. Winter.

L. autumnalis Conical pseudobulbs with two to three leaves. Flowers one to ten, bright rose purple, white in the centre. Autumn.

L. gouldiana Similar to *L. autumnalis*, but flowers smaller.

L. rubescens Compressed and wrinkled pseudobulbs with one leaf. Flowers eight to twelve, white to pale pink or lavender, with a dark blotch on the lip. Winter.

L. speciosa (*L. grandiflora*) Small, squat pseudobulbs with one to three leaves appearing after flowering. Flowers one to four, pale rose purple, lovely. Spring.

× *LAELIOCATTLEYA (Lc.)*

Some of the most striking and brilliantly coloured hybrids in the *Cattleya* alliance are actually intergeneric crosses, *Laelia* × *Cattleya*, which are known as × *Laeliocattleya (Lc.)*. They are strong, robust plants which require the same growing conditions as cattleyas. Recommended hybrids are Amber Glow and Edgard van Belle (yellow/orange with a red lip), Drumbeat and Culminant 'La Tuilerie' (large pink/lavender with purple lip), Amacynth (white with purple lip), Chitchat 'Tangerine' (small, bright orange flowers), Jay Markell (white), and Ann Follis (green with purple lip). There are many others.

LEMBOGLOSSUM

These pretty dwarf epiphytes were until quite recently included in the genus *Odontoglossum*. They all have rounded or ovoid pseudobulbs, clustered together, with one to three terminal leaves. The flowers are showy, white, pink or yellow, and brown, often spotted or barred.

Most species come from high altitudes in Mexico and Central America, where a pronounced dry and cooler season alternates with a warm, wet summer. In cultivation they grow best in shallow pots or mounted on bark slabs. Cool.

L. apterum Pseudobulbs with two leaves. Flowers four to six, on new growths, white with brown spots at the base of all the parts. Early spring.

L. bictoniense Pseudobulbs slightly compressed, with one to three apical leaves. Flowers ten to twenty on a long, erect spike, greenish or brownish with a white or pink lip.

L. cervantesii Pseudobulbs grey-green, compressed, with one apical leaf. Flowers two to eight, pink or white with concentric, broken, brown rings at the base of the parts. Flowers last for some weeks during the winter, though they look fragile.

L. cordatum Pseudobulbs compressed, with one apical leaf. Flowers five to ten, greenish yellow, heavily barred with brown, lip white and also spotted. Spring.

L. maculatum Similar to the above but with shorter petals and a yellow lip. Autumn or winter.

L. rossii Similar to *L. cervantesii* but spotted on the sepals and the base of the petals. Winter.

LUDISIA

This well-known representative of the jewel orchids is widespread in China and southeast Asia and is widely cultivated. Most of the group have rather insignificant flowers, but in **L. discolor**, the only species in the genus, the bright white and yellow flowers are held erect above the dark reddish green leaves, where they show up well and provide a pleasing contrast.

In the wild, the creeping stems grow across the surface of the forest floor, rooting at the nodes. Each stem turns upright after a short distance and bears a number of petiolate leaves that are dark reddish purple and have attractive gold veining.

Under good conditions of high humidity, deep shade and warm temperatures, plants grow strongly and will form an attractive carpet, quickly covering the shallow pans in which they are best grown. A peat-based but freely draining compost is most suitable. Plants require plenty of water, dilute fertilizer and good ventilation throughout the year. Single growths are often sold as pot plants as a result of the successful large-scale propagation of this orchid by tissue culture techniques.

LYCASTE

About 25 species of these cool-growing orchids are known from the Americas, from Mexico south to Peru and Bolivia. They have large plicate leaves that distinguish them from *Maxillaria*. In both genera the flowers have large sepals and are borne singly on peduncles arising from the base of the plant.

The plants need cool conditions with good air movement throughout the year. They take up a lot of space when in their leafy summer growth, but it is worth having a few lycastes in a collection for their attractive, long-lasting flowers. Cool.

L. aromatica A Mexican species that has bright yellow flowers in great quantity. Winter or early spring.

L. crinita Both this and *L. cruenta* are rather similar to *L. aromatica*. Spring.

L. denningiana A striking species from Ecuador. The green flowers on tall peduncles have a bright orange lip. Winter.

L. deppei This Mexican species has large flowers on rather short stalks. They have pale green sepals dotted with red, white petals and a yellow lip. Winter.

L. lasioglossa A species from Guatemala, which has orange-red flowers with a yellow lip on tall peduncles. Winter and spring.

L. macrophylla A very floriferous species from Peru. Green flowers with a pink-spotted white lip. Winter and early spring.

L. skinneri (*L. virginalis*) The national flower of Guatemala and always a favourite species. Flowers in various shades of white, pink or rose, usually with a darker lip. Winter or early spring.

L. tricolor A small flowered species from Guatemala. The flowers are a greenish tan with white petals and a white, pink-spotted lip. Summer.

Opposite:
Miltoniopsis Saint Brelade, a hybrid bred from *M. roezlii* at the Eric Young Orchid Foundation, Jersey (see page 98)
Below: *Lycaste* Wyldfire 'Blaze of Tara' AM/RHS (see page 96)

Hybrids Many beautiful hybrids have been developed over the years, mostly with larger and brighter flowers than the species. Recommended hybrids are Auburn (many shades of pink and red), Jason (gold with a red lip), Koolena (white, shell pink and reddish), Shoalhaven (pink), Wyldfire (dark red), Vulcan (red) and Concentration (yellow).

MASDEVALLIA

These dwarf epiphytes are cool-growing and very popular with orchid lovers. Many of them flower throughout the year, whenever a new leafy growth is mature. They come from the highlands of the New World, from Mexico south to Peru, with the greatest number in the Andes. Plants grow in tufts with each slender stem bearing a single leaf. The sepals are the most conspicuous part of the flower, often united at the base to form a tube and with the free ends extending to form long, slender, pointed tails. The small petals and lip are usually hidden within the flower.

These orchids are easy to grow in a greenhouse. They need small pots with a peat- or bark-based compost that is compact but drains freely. They need water and fertilizer throughout the year, and conditions that are shady and humid with good air movement. Cool.

M. calocodon Unusual cream or pink flowers, striped with maroon or brown. Summer.

M. caudata A Colombian species with attractive pink flowers with long yellow tails. Summer.

M. coccinea Pretty pink, rose or crimson flowers, from Colombia. Spring. Other very striking red-flowered species with slightly smaller flowers are *M. amabilis*, *M. harryana*, *M. ignea*, *M. racemosa*, *M. stumpflei* and *M. welischii*.

M. colossus Large reddish brown flowers, two or three to each peduncle. Autumn.

M. estradae Brightly coloured, yellow and magenta flowers. Colombia. Summer.

M. glandulosa Small but brilliantly coloured rose flowers with darker spots, clove scented. Autumn.

M. polysticta Several flowers on each elongated raceme, white with purple spots and yellow tails. Peru. Winter and spring.

M. prodigiosa Pale, peach-coloured pink flowers with a widely flaring tube. Recently described from Peru. Winter and spring.

M. reichenbachiana A species from Costa Rica. Flowers with a lovely contrast of pearly white and polished mahogany. Summer.

M. strobelii Flowers white and golden orange with long orange tails, the inside of the sepals densely hairy. Autumn.

M. uniflora A delicate and elegant flower, silvery white, suffused with purple above the middle or along the margins. Autumn.

M. veitchiana A most spectacular species, with brilliant orange-scarlet flowers that have broad bands of purple papillae forming a streak across each sepal. Spring and summer.

Hybrids Many interesting hybrids were made at the turn of the century, and this activity has been started again in the last 20 years. Many are showy and very floriferous. Some recommended hybrids are Diana (white with red stripes, yellow tails), Doris (orange), Kimballiana (burnt orange), Marguerite (coppery orange), Prince Charming (large flowers, orange, with red stripes), Shuttryana (deep rose cerise) and Snowbird (white).

MAXILLARIA

This is a large genus from tropical and subtropical America, with more than 300 species. The plants are extremely varied in shape and size, with long or short rhizomes and large or small pseudobulbs each bearing one or two tough, folded leaves. Inflorescences arise in clusters from the base of the pseudobulb, or singly, and each bears a solitary flower, yellow, brown, red, white or mottled. The sepals are usually longer than the petals, and the lateral sepals form a distinct pouch, or mentum, where they enclose the base of the lip.

Most species grow well in pots or baskets in a bark-based compost. Plants grow naturally in a wide range of habitats, so a selection can be made to suit a wide range of temperature conditions in cultivation.

M. camaridii This species has long, sprawling stems with scattered pseudobulbs. The waxy white flowers are 5 cm (2 in) across and scented like narcissus, but last only for a day. Spring.

M. coccinea A dwarf species from the Antilles, which has bright red flowers of up to 2 cm (nearly 1 in) across. Summer.

M. juergensii A dwarf species with tiny pseudobulbs and erect, fleshy leaves. The flowers are dark reddish brown with a lip of shiny maroon. Autumn.

M. macrura Each rhizome bears a row of compressed pseudobulbs, each producing several flowers. They are up to 12 cm (5 in) across, pinkish tan in colour.

M. picta A varied species from Brazil, with strap-shaped leaves and many solitary flowers. They are whitish on the outside with dark red spots, yellow within. Winter. Other recommended yellow-and-brown-flowered species include *M. parkeri*, *M. consanguinea*, *M. marginata*, *M. multiflora*, *M. ochroleuca* and *M. punctata*, all from Brazil.

M. sanderiana This is considered to be the finest of the genus, and comes from Ecuador. The flowers are 10–15 cm (4–6 in) across, white, marked with blood red, on erect or drooping stems. Autumn.

M. tenuifolia The coconut orchid from Mexico has round or egg-shaped pseudobulbs on a creeping rhizome. The long, grass-like leaves tend to hide the brownish red flowers, which are 2.5–4 cm (1–1½ in) across and have a characteristic scent. Spring to autumn.

M. valenzuelana (*M. iridifolia*) A pendulous epiphyte with several leaves arranged in the shape of a fan. Flowers yellow, up to 2.5 cm (1 in) across. Summer.

MILTONIA

A Brazilian genus with about 20 species, which are separated from *Miltoniopsis* by their two-leaved pseudobulbs and winged column. There are few or many flowers in a slender raceme, usually large and brightly coloured.

These plants are often rather spreading, and grow well in shallow pots or baskets in a bark-based compost. They need shade, high humidity and plenty of water while growing, followed by a drier period during the winter. Intermediate.

M. clowesii Large sprays of flowers. The front of the lip is white, the sepals and petals golden brown, blotched with chestnut. Spring.

M. cuneata Rather similar to *M. clowesii*, but the whole of the lip is pure white. Spring.

M. flavescens Sprays of pale yellow, starry flowers, rather similar to some of the brassias. Summer.

M. spectabilis A variety of colour forms is known for this showy species – white, rose and dark purple. The flowers are large and flat, and there are only one to three on each inflorescence. The colour of the lip and its darker venation provide a lovely contrast with the rest of the flower. Autumn.

Hybrids These warm-growing miltonias have been used in a number of crosses with other genera, e.g. *Brassia* to make × *Miltassia* (× *Mtssa.*), and *Odontoglossum* to make × *Odontonia* (× *Odtna.*). Recommended hybrids are × *Mtssa.* Charles M. Fitch, Citron, Limbo Dancers; × *Odtna.* Brown Sugar, Debutante, Diane.

MILTONIOPSIS

There are five species of pansy orchids in the mountains of Costa Rica, Panama, Venezuela, Colombia and Ecuador. Their clustered pale green pseudobulbs are com-

Masdevallia strobelii from Ecuador (see page 96)

pressed, two-edged, and bear only a single leaf at the apex. The short racemes bear large, rather flat flowers in shades of pink, red, white and pale yellow. They make delightful pot plants but do not last well as cut flowers.

Plants grow best in small pots in a shaded and humid situation where there is plenty of fresh air movement. The compost should be free-draining but may be peat- or bark-based. Mostly intermediate.

M. phalaenopsis A cool-growing species from Colombia. Flowers white with a handsome four-lobed lip that is streaked with red spots in the form of 'tear drops'. Late spring.

M. roezlii This species from Colombia and Panama has a conspicuous purple blotch at the base of each petal. Autumn.

M. vexillaria This is the prettiest species, and comes from Colombia. It is white, pale pink or deep rose, and has a prominent yellow crest at the base of the lip. Spring.

Hybrids Many hybrids have been produced. Their flowers are larger and more colourful than those of the wild species. The plants are often more tolerant of varying conditions in cultivation than the wild ones, and mostly flower in early summer. Recommended hybrids are Emotion (pink), Hamburg, Storm and Gordon Hoyt (red), Toby Strauss (pastel shades).

Miltoniopsis Hamburg 'Stonehurst' AM/RHS

× ODONTIODA (Oda.)

The earliest of the many intergeneric crosses in the *Oncidium* alliance, the cross between *Odontoglossum* and *Cochlioda* was first recorded in 1904. The bright rose-pink and scarlet flowered species of *Cochlioda* have contributed their lovely colours to make the larger flowered odontiodas, including a number of strikingly beautiful hybrids. They are easily grown under the same cool conditions as the parents. Recommended hybrids are Bradshawiae, Chanticleer, Charlesworthii, Heatonensis, Keighleyensis, Nicola, Picasso. When these have been further bred with large flowered *Odontoglossum* hybrids, some very beautiful colour combinations have resulted. The following × *Odontioda* grexes include some outstanding cultivars: Brocade, Dalmar, Florence Stirling, Ingera, Joe Marshall, Red Rum, Salway, Trixon.

ODONTOGLOSSUM

There are now considered to be about 60 species of cool-growing orchids in this Central and South American genus. They are mostly epiphytic plants with round or ovoid, compressed pseudobulbs bearing one to three leaves. The inflorescence is basal, with one to many colourful flowers.

Many of the species grow at high altitudes in the wild, so they need cool

temperatures, and not more than 25°C (75°F) in summer. Fresh, moving air around the plants is essential, but the roots should not be allowed to become dry. Plants grow best in plastic pots in a free-draining compost which may be peat- or bark-based. Cool.

O. cirrhosum A species from Ecuador, with milky white flowers with purplish brown spots on long acuminate sepals and petals, and a golden base to the lip. The inflorescence is simple or branched with many flowers. Spring.

O. crispum The best-known species from Colombia, whose flowers may be pure sparkling white or with various amounts of yellow or reddish spots. In cultivation many improved forms of this species have been raised by selective breeding. Spring.

O. hallii A species from Ecuador and Peru with brown and gold flowers except for the lip, which is white in the outer third with a frilly margin. Four to twenty flowers are borne on long sprays. Spring.

O. luteopurpureum A species from Colombia with long, slender inflorescences. Flowers golden yellow, with reddish brown spots and blotches that are heaviest on the sepals. Spring.

O. odoratum (*O. gloriosum*) This species from Venezuela has many yellow flowers, with few small red spots on long, acuminate sepals and petals, on branching inflorescences. Spring.

O. ramosissimum A Colombian species with long sprays of many pale pink flowers, which have crimson markings and a crimson crest on the lip. Spring.

Hybrids Many hybrids have been made with members of this genus since the earliest days of orchid-growing. They have also been bred with the red-flowered cochliodas to produce bright red and yellow cultivars of × *Odontioda* (× *Oda.*), which are always popular (see page 98).

Other intergeneric crosses of *Odontoglossum* which produce cool-growing plants that are easy to grow are × *Odontonia* (× *Odtna.*, with *Miltonia* or *Miltoniopsis*), × *Odontocidium* (× *Odcdm.*, with *Oncidium*), and some multigeneric hybrids including × *Wilsonara* (× *Wils.*, with *Cochlioda* and *Oncidium*) (see page 113) and × *Vuylstekeara* (× *Vuyl.*, with *Cochlioda* and *Miltonia* or *Miltoniopsis*) (see page 113).

ONCIDIUM

This colourful genus is one of the largest in cultivation, with more than 500 species in the American tropics. The 'dancing lady'

× *Odontocidium*
Tiger Butter

Oncidium varicosum
from Brazil (see page 101)

flowers are instantly recognizable, each with a four-lobed lip held at a right angle to the column, and with a conspicuous callus in its basal half. The plants themselves are extremely diverse in shape and size, and growing conditions for them vary accordingly.

Nearly all the plants require a brightly lit situation, with shade from direct sunlight only during the summer. Some grow best when mounted on tree fern fibre or a bark slab, others in a pot or basket. All need plenty of water and fertilizer during the growing season.

FAN-SHAPED PLANTS

These small plants of the Variegata section of the genus are known from their growth habit as the equitant oncidiums. Each plant consists of a small, iris-like fan of leaves with overlapping bases. They require humid but buoyant conditions, and minimum night temperatures of 12–15°C (55–60°F). Well-grown species, and some of the colourful hybrids bred from them, flower on wiry stems during the summer and sometimes throughout the year. Flowers up to 2.5 cm (1 in) across.

O. pulchellum A species from Jamaica and the West Indies that has branching inflorescences of white, pink or deep rose flowers.

O. urophyllum Also from the West Indies, this species has yellow flowers with a red and white crest on the lip.

O. variegatum Found in South Florida and the West Indies, this species has long sprays of flowers, from white to lavender.

Hybrids Many hybrids have been made among this group in recent years. They are easily grown on a warm windowsill, and flower frequently. Recommended hybrids in many different colours are Spanish Lady, Golden Sunset, William Thurston, Red Velvet and Royal Purple.

THIN-LEAVED SPECIES

A large number of *Oncidium* species have clusters of pseudobulbs each bearing one or

two leaves at the apex. Many of these are easily grown in cultivation in cool, warm or intermediate temperatures, and they mostly flower during the summer months.

O. cheirophorum Small plants from Colombia, with branching inflorescences of many small, greenish yellow flowers. Scented.

O. crispum A brown and gold species from Brazil. The large flowers have a crispate margin to the petals and lip.

O. flexuosum Small plants from Brazil with long sprays, up to 1 m (3 ft), of small chestnut and yellow flowers each with a large canary yellow lip.

O. globuliferum A scrambling species from Colombia, with rounded pseudobulbs some way apart on a creeping rhizome and each bearing single, large, golden flowers.

O. incurvum From Mexico, huge, branching sprays of small flowers on small plants. The lip is mostly white and the rest of the flower has rose dots on a white ground. Cool-growing.

O. leucochilum Large plants. The flowers are reddish brown and yellow with a white lip.

O. maculatum These winter-flowering plants from Mexico have large sprays of widely separated flowers. The lip is pale yellow with a crimson crest, the rest of the flower pale yellow with brown spots.

O. ornithorhynchum A very floriferous species from Mexico and Guatemala, with many sweetly scented flowers on branching inflorescences. Flowers pink or, rarely, white, during the winter months. Cool-growing.

O. sphacelatum A commonly grown species that originally came from Mexico and Guatemala. It has many chestnut and gold flowers on long, branching inflorescences.

O. tigrinum A winter-flowering species from Mexico that has green sepals and petals barred with brown, and a bright yellow lip.

O. varicosum One of the prettiest species, from Brazil, with small sepals and petals and a very large bright yellow lip, often with a reddish stain in front of the crest.

THICK-LEAVED SPECIES

In this group of *Oncidium* species from tropical America the pseudobulbs are scarcely visible, and each is surmounted by a thick leaf shaped like a mule's ear. They like warm conditions, with minimum night temperatures of 15°C (60°F). Summer flowering.

O. carthagenense The leaves are red-spotted and the thick inflorescences bear many small flowers, yellowish white, spotted with lavender, magenta or red.

O. cavendishianum Very similar to the above but the flowers are brilliant yellow, with only the sepals and petals spotted with dark reddish brown.

O. lanceanum An uncommon species from Trinidad and Guyana. The large, fragrant flowers are yellowish green, spotted with brown, and with a brilliant rose purple lip.

O. splendidum This Mexican species has larger pseudobulbs than the others in the group, each with a thick leaf. The flower spikes are sometimes 2 m (6 ft) tall, with many large flowers. It is sometimes known as the tiger orchid because the yellow sepals and petals are barred with brown. The large lip is pure yellow.

PENCIL-LEAVED SPECIES

Several species have elongated rounded leaves, which are usually pendent from the small pseudobulbs. Sometimes known as the rat-tail orchids, they grow best when mounted on a slab of cork oak bark.

O. cebolleta Flowers with a bright yellow lip and brown spotted sepals and petals.

O. jonesianum Similar to *O. cebolleta*, but with a clear white lip.

Hybrids Many hybrids have been made and grown, particularly among the equitant oncidiums. *Oncidium* species have also been used as a parent in many intergeneric crosses, often contributing their floriferous habit, as well as brown and gold colours, to the resulting progeny. They can all be grown in intermediate or cool night temperatures. The most frequently cultivated examples of these hybrids are × *Aliceara* (× *Alcra.*: *Brassia* × *Miltonia* × *Oncidium*); × *Colmanara* (× *Colm.*: *Odontoglossum* × *Miltonia* × *Oncidium*); × *Maclellanara* (× *Mclna.*: *Brassia* × *Oncidium* × *Odontoglossum*); × *Odontocidium* (× *Odcdm.*: *Odontoglossum* × *Oncidium*); and × *Wilsonara* (× *Wils.*: *Odontoglossum* × *Oncidium* × *Cochlioda*).

OPHRYS

There are about 50 species and many distinct varieties in the bee orchid group, mostly in the Mediterranean region. Four can be found in Britain. In late winter a new rosette of leaves is produced from the underground tubers, from which the flowering stem emerges in spring or early summer. They are curious plants in that the flowers resemble the females of different species of insect, and have developed a very specialized pollination mechanism. Male insects are deceived by them, and transport the pollinia from one flower to another whilst attempting copulatory activities.

The bee orchids grow in calcareous soils at a number of grassland sites, but they are not easy to establish or maintain in gardens. A few species are available from specialist bulb growers and can be grown as alpines, both in the rock garden and in an unheated greenhouse. A freely draining compost is essential, and most plants need a long dry period after flowering until the new growth is well developed.

Many of the species are extremely variable, and there are also a great number of natural hybrids in the wild. These facts make the recognition and naming of species in this group very difficult.

O. apifera The English bee orchid, which has pink sepals and petals, and a brown and green hairy lip.

O. lutea An early flowering species with bright greenish yellow flowers. The lip is bright golden yellow with a brownish central part. Widespread in the Mediterranean region.

O. tenthredinifera This is one of the largest species, with spectacular pink, brown and yellow flowers. Widespread in the Mediterranean area.

O. vernixia (*O. speculum*) A dark flower with a brilliant bluish patch, like a mirror, surrounded by blackish hairs on the lip.

ORCHIS

These were the first terrestrial orchids to be described by Linnaeus, and their name is used for the family. They have underground tubers from which a new rosette of leaves and a flowering shoot arise annually, producing flowers in late spring and summer. The lip, which is spurred at the base, is the most distinctive part of the flower.

Although not often cultivated, a few species are grown as alpines, usually in pots in an unheated greenhouse, and a few survive in rock gardens, in rough grassland or even in lawns.

O. mascula The early purple orchid is found in Europe and Asia. It has stems up to 45 cm (18 in) high and purple-spotted leaves. The flowers are borne in dense spikes, pinkish mauve with darker spots.

O. morio The green winged orchid has green or spotted leaves and rather few pale magenta flowers on short stems. It grows on clay and on calcareous soils, and is present in great numbers on a few lawns in English gardens.

O. papilionacea Found in countries bordering the western end of the Mediterranean. Leaves green, without spots. The flowers have deep pinkish brown sepals and petals, and a large pale pink lip with darker stripes or rows of small spots.

OSMOGLOSSUM

Formerly included in the genus *Odontoglossum*, this is a small group of

Orchis morio decorating a wild flower lawn in Dorset, England

about seven species in the highlands of Mexico and Guatemala.

O. pulchellum The best-known species is widely grown for its waxy white flowers, which are borne in profusion during late autumn and winter. Each flower is 2–5 cm ($\frac{3}{4}$–2 in) across, and is carried with the lip uppermost on the spike. As for the odontoglossums, cool-growing conditions are necessary.

PAPHIOPEDILUM

The tropical slipper orchids from Asia are very popular in cultivation. More than 60 species have been described, but only about 20 of these are commonly grown. There are also many hybrids available in a wide range of colours.

They are terrestrial herbs, occasionally growing on rocks or trees. The plants have a short rhizome from which upright fans of leaves arise, usually close together, which are either medium green in colour or attractively tessellated with dark and light green, sometimes purple-tinged. The waxy flowers are borne singly, successively or a few together on an erect inflorescence. The dorsal sepal is erect, often spotted or striped, and the lateral sepals are united behind the slipper-shaped lip. The petals are usually narrow and

spreading, sometimes with hairy warts along the margin.

All the plants, species and hybrids, grow best in a freely draining compost which is changed annually. These slipper orchids have no water storage organs and are some of the few orchids that should not be allowed to dry out. Plastic pots are therefore the best containers, and a humid, shady greenhouse the best place for them. Those with variegated leaves require more shade and warmth than the plain green kinds.

COOL-GROWING SPECIES

P. fairrieanum A species from India, Bhutan and Sikkim with small, rather quaint flowers, white striped with dark red or, rarely, with green. Autumn.

P. insigne A species from India and Nepal with a wide range of colour forms, mostly in shades of gold and brown with a spotted dorsal sepal. Autumn. Recommended varieties are var. *sanderae*, plain greeny gold with a white margin to the dorsal sepal, no spots; and var. *insigne* 'Harefield Hall', a very large flowered form, pinkish brown on the dorsal sepal with a white margin and very heavy chocolate spots.

P. spicerianum A small flowered species from India and Burma. The flowers are yellowish green, with a conspicuous pur-

Ophrys apifera from England (see page 101)

Paphiopedilum spicerianum from India

ple staminode and a dark stripe across the centre of the white dorsal sepal. Early winter.

P. villosum A widespread species from India, Burma and Thailand. The overall colour is gingery brown, sometimes lighter or darker, but the most conspicuous feature is the polished appearance of the sepals and lip. There are many colour variants. Winter.

WARM-GROWING SPECIES

P. barbatum A species from Malaysia with variegated leaves. The flowers are white and purple with hairy warts along the upper margin of the petals. Winter to spring.

P. callosum A species very similar to *P. barbatum*, from Thailand, Cambodia and Laos, but with larger flowers. Early summer.

P. concolor A widespread species with mottled leaves, from southwest China (Yunnan) south to Thailand and Vietnam. This is a small species that is often lithophytic in nature. Each growth bears one or two pale yellow flowers with small purplish spots. Late autumn.

P. delenatii This pink-and-white-flowered slipper orchid was introduced to France from Vietnam in 1913. It has now become widespread in collections as a result of propagations from seeds of that introduction and from subsequent matings. Spring.

P. haynaldianum A large species from the Philippines. It is sometimes lithophytic or epiphytic, and its long green leaves are thick and leathery. There are usually three or four elegant flowers on a tall inflorescence, greenish yellow with dark maroon spots on the basal half of the sepals, and the petals a pretty pinkish purple in the outer half. Spring.

P. parishii A multiflowered species from Burma, Thailand and southwest China that is usually epiphytic. Flowers two to nine, light green and brown with slender, spirally twisted petals. Summer.

P. primulinum A pretty species from Sumatra with small, clear yellow flowers that appear successively over a period of several months. The leaves are narrow and dull green. Spring.

P. rothschildianum A very handsome species from Borneo, which is a great rarity in the wild but easily propagated from seed in cultivation. The inflorescence stands erect, with two to five large flowers, which are pale green or yellowish and striped purple, above plain green leaves. Early summer.

P. sukhakulii A distinctive species from northern Thailand with tessellated foliage. The flowers are green and brown with heavily spotted petals. It grows quickly and easily and has become quite common in cultivation. Autumn.

Hybrids Since the first man-made hybrid, *P.* Harrisianum, flowered in 1869, a very large number of crosses have been made among the slipper orchids. They are easy to raise from seed, to grow and to flower, and more hybrids have been registered in this one group of orchids than in any other. A wide range of shapes, sizes and colours is now available. They grow best at intermediate temperatures, and flower during the winter and spring. Recommended hybrids are Whitemoor 'Snowy', Silvara, Susan Tucker and F.C. Puddle (white); Vanda M. Pearman, Aladin and Darling (pink); Diana Broughton, Sunwillow, Ambrosia, Honey Gorse, Kay Rinaman and Tommie Hanes (yellow/green); Hellas, Sarella and Tangold (orange); Brownstone, Danella and Amanda (brown); Redstart, Orchilla 'Chilton', Royale, St Alban (red); Winston Churchill 'Indomitable', British Bulldog and Cameo (spotted); Maudiae, Claire de Lune and Makuli (green and white striped); Vintner's Treasure and Dragon's Blood (dark crimson); Transvaal, Shireen, Vanguard and St Swithin (*P. rothschildianum* hybrids).

PHAIUS

These terrestrial orchids have very large plicate leaves and take up a lot of space in a small greenhouse, but the plants are very rewarding. Their tall inflorescences continue in flower over a long period. They need large plastic pots to accommodate their pseudobulbs and large root systems in a freely draining compost. High humidity and good air movement are desirable, but a wide range of temperatures is tolerated.

P. callosus These large plants in the Princess of Wales Conservatory at the Royal Botanic Gardens, Kew are almost always in flower. They have large leaves, and tall spikes with pink and red flowers. Intermediate.

P. tankervilleae The nun orchid has drooping flowers that are white on the outside but a rich brown on the inner surface. The lip is rosy pink. It is widespread, from northern India and China south to Australia, and was one of the earliest tropical orchids to flower in Europe. Intermediate, spring.

PHALAENOPSIS

The moth orchids are Asiatic plants that are very popular for their attractive and long-lasting flowers. Some of the newer hybrids are proving suitable as pot plants in centrally heated homes.

The plants are epiphytic in the wild. They have no pseudobulbs but many aerial roots and succulent leaves. Moth orchids grow best in a bark-based compost in pots or slatted baskets. They need a shady greenhouse with high humidity where they can be watered and fertilized frequently. Intermediate or warm.

P. amabilis (*P. grandiflora*) One of the earliest known of the epiphytic orchids. The leaves are shiny green and fleshy, the flowers white with long tails on the lip and a golden yellow callus. Winter.

P. lueddemanniana A very varied species from the Philippines. The star-shaped flowers are creamy yellow with brown or purple markings, bars or spots, and a bright carmine lip. Various times.

P. pulchra Another Philippines species, of similar shape to *P. lueddemanniana*, but with flowers of a brilliant magenta-purple. Spring.

P. schilleriana This Philippines (Luzon) species has attractive silver-mottled foliage, and huge branching sprays of many pink and white flowers. Winter, and at other times.

P. stuartiana Also from the Philippines (Mindanao), this white-flowered species has similar foliage. It differs from *P. amabilis* in the cinnamon-coloured spots on the lower half of the lateral sepals. Winter.

P. violacea There are lovely star-shaped flowers on this green-leaved species from Sumatra, Borneo and Malaysia. The flowers are fleshy, pale green but flushed with purple in the central parts. Summer.

Hybrids Many hybrids have been developed from these and other species. They grow quickly and easily in warm conditions, and reach flowering size from seed in two to three years. A wide range of colours is available and the flowers are long-lasting. Recommended hybrids are Henriette Lecoufle, Grace Palm, Alice Gloria, Winter Maiden and Cast Iron Monarch (white); Hokuspokus, Romance, Zauberrose and Jane Almquist (pink); Tyler Carlson and Golden Buddha (yellow); Painted Cave, Sarah Frances Pridgen and Sweet Dreams (spotted); Red Eye and Redfan (white with coloured lip).

PHRAGMIPEDIUM

The Central and South American slipper orchids are mostly robust plants that grow on dripping rock faces; a few are epiphytic. They produce large groups of fans of tough green leaves, each fan terminating its growth with a tall inflorescence.

The plants need a freely draining compost but should be kept moist throughout the year. They flower best if kept in fairly bright light with high humidity throughout the year. Intermediate.

P. besseae A species recently discovered in Peru and Ecuador, with brilliant orange-scarlet flowers on small growths. Autumn.

Phalaenopsis Sarah
Frances Pridgen
(see page 105) at
the Eric Young
Orchid
Foundation, Jersey

buds appear first, and the leaves, one or two, develop after the flowers. Roots are put forth from the base of the leafy shoot. As soon as they appear the plants need plenty of water and fertilizer until the leaves turn yellow and fall in the autumn. Then the pots must be kept completely dry and cool for several months. They are repotted annually in a freely draining compost, before or after flowering. They are best grown as alpines in an unheated greenhouse, or a very cool one, and some species may prove hardy in a sheltered corner of the rock garden.

Pleiones are also known as 'windowsill orchids' because they can be grown with very little trouble among other pot plants. By choosing a suitable mixture of species and hybrids, a careful grower could have some plants in flower from October through to May.

AUTUMN-FLOWERING SPECIES

P. maculata From India, Burma and Thailand. The pseudobulbs are green and maroon, covered with small white warts, and bear two leaves. The flowers are basically creamy white with dark purple blotches on the lip.

P. praecox One of the first species collected, and now known from China, India, Nepal and Burma. The pseudobulbs are maroon, covered with greenish warts, and two leaved. The flowers are usually pinkish purple, the lip with darker blotches and yellow lamellae.

P. caudatum An extremely large and unusual orchid that is widespread from Guatemala south to Peru. The flowers are pale green, with darker venation and narrow pinkish petals. The petals gradually elongate after the flowers open, eventually becoming 40 cm (16 in) or more long. Autumn.

P. longifolium The most common species in cultivation, and easy to grow. It is widespread between Costa Rica and Ecuador. The inflorescence bears many flowers one at a time over a long period; the flowers are pale green, the petals edged with purple. Flowers throughout the year.

P. Sedenii A handsome hybrid between P. schlimii and P. longifolium, first raised by Seden more than 100 years ago. The plants are robust, quick and easy growers, and almost always in flower. The attractive pink and white blooms last two to four weeks.

PLEIONE

Sometimes known as the Himalayan crocuses, these pretty orchids are mostly terrestrial and come from high mountains between Nepal and Taiwan. The little plants make a new growth every year from the old, onion-shaped pseudobulb. Flower

Pleione humilis
from India

White *Phalaenopsis* hybrids and pink *P. schilleriana* in a display to represent Mount Fuji at the 12th World Orchid Conference in Tokyo, Japan (see page 105)

SPRING-FLOWERING SPECIES

P. bulbocodioides A widespread species from China and Tibet. The pseudobulbs are dark green, pointed and one leaved, and the flowers a rich rose-pink with orange spots on the lip.

P. formosana A species from eastern China and Taiwan that has often been confused with *P. bulbocodioides* but differs in flower colour, the lip being paler than the rest of the flower with a broad yellow band as well as orange spots. This is the most common species in cultivation, and many clones have received cultivar names. Some are almost hardy. Recommended cultivars are 'Blush of Dawn', 'Oriental Grace', 'Oriental Splendour' and 'Purple Emperor' (petals in shades of pink or lilac); 'Clare' and 'Snow White' (large white flowers, often two per stem).

P. humilis One of the earliest species collected, from India, Nepal and Burma. Pseudobulbs green, smooth, one-leaved.

Flowers white, lip heavily spotted with purple or orange.

Hybrids A number of pretty hybrids have been bred in the last 20 years and are now available from specialists. Their flowering period can be controlled by shortening or prolonging the cool, dry season, so that flowers are available through the late winter and spring. Recommended hybrids are Alishan (lilac, lip white with red spots); Stromboli (deep rose-purple throughout, lip with orange spots); Shantung (pale yellow with deeper yellow lip, blotched dark red); Tongariro (various shades of purple, lip marked with red and yellow); Versailles (very pale rosy mauve with slightly darker markings on the lip).

PLEUROTHALLIS

This is one of the largest genera in the family, with more than 900 species in tropical America. The plants have small flowers, which are often produced in great abundance at the top of slender, one-leaved stems. By far the greatest number of species come from montane areas, so they need moist, humid and cool conditions in cultivation.

Plants grow best in small pots or baskets or mounted on tree fern fibre, and need water throughout the year. Cool.

P. grobyi Small plants, 7–10 cm (3–4 in) tall, from Mexico to South America. Many flowers are produced; they are bright yellow streaked with crimson. Summer.

P. pterophora Small plants up to 10 cm (4 in) tall from Brazil. Very floriferous with sparkling white, bell-shaped flowers in elongated spikes reminiscent of lily of the valley. Flowers throughout the year.

P. racemiflora A small species that is widespread from Jamaica and Mexico south to Venezuela. The plants are 10–15 cm (4–6 in) tall and bear long sprays of tiny yellowish green flowers. Autumn.

P. roezlii A tall species from Colombia, up to 40 cm (16 in) tall. Flowers large, deep blackish purple, the lip covered with white hairs. Spring.

P. schiedii (*P. ornata*) A tiny species from Mexico and Guatemala, only 2.5–5 cm (1–2 in) tall. The flowers are pale purplish brown, the margins of the sepals bearing white pendants of wax that move in the slightest draught. Various times.

× POTINARA (Pot.)

The members of this group of colourful hybrids have a complex ancestry, with representatives of four different genera involved in their breeeding – *Brassavola*, *Cattleya*, *Laelia* and *Sophronitis*. Nearly all the progeny have smaller flowers than the laeliocattleyas or brassocattleyas, but the best red and orange colours, as well as some fine yellows, are found among them. Intermediate. Recommended hybrids are Tapestry Peak and Fortune Teller (yellow); Rebecca Merkel, Red Dip and Amangi 'Orchidglade' (red); Fuschia Fantasy (magenta).

PROMENAEA

This small Brazilian genus is easily recognized by its greyish green leaves and pseudobulbs, and rather large flowers on the small plants. In the wild the plants are epiphytic, and they are best grown in shallow pots with a freely draining compost. Shady and humid conditions suit them well, but it is important to grow the plants where there is plenty of fresh air movement as the growths rot easily if they remain wet for too long. Cool.

P. stapelioides Flowers usually single, cream or pale brown but so heavily marked with maroon spots that they appear blackish purple. Summer.

P. xanthina (*P. citrina*) Flowers usually solitary, bright citron yellow. Summer.

PSYCHOPSIS

The tropical butterfly orchids have often been included in the genus *Oncidium*, but the four or five species are now usually recognized as distinct. They have a creeping growth habit, with the one-leaved pseudobulbs erect or flattened against the surface over which they are growing. The solitary flowers are borne on long, slender inflorescences and are immediately recognizable by their slender sepals, broad petals and frilly lip. They are all yellow and orange brown.

These plants need warm, humid and shady conditions in cultivation. They grow well mounted on tree fern fibre or in shallow pots with a freely draining compost. Warm.

P. krameriana Widespread from Costa Rica to Ecuador at low altitudes, with flowers that are large and showy, and appear successively over a long period, one or two at a time on a rounded stalk. Various times.

P. papilio Widespread from Trinidad to Peru in the lower montane forests. The flowers are large and showy, produced one at a time on a flattened stalk, appearing successively over a long period. Various times.

RENANTHERA

The red, yellow and orange flowers of these large Asiatic orchids are extremely showy. The plants are very tall, however, and do not flower readily in temperate northern greenhouses. They need bright light, high humidity and warm temperatures at all times. They grow well in pots or baskets suspended from the roof of the greenhouse with their abundant aerial roots hanging free. Warm.

R. coccinea A scrambling, long-stemmed plant from India and Burma. Inflorescences large, often branching, with orange-red flowers covered with darker red spots. Autumn.

R. monachica One of the smaller species from the Philippines. The simple racemes bear many flowers, which are yellow dotted with red. Winter to spring.

RHYNCHOSTYLIS

About six species of fox tail orchids are known from Asia. This monopodial genus is easily recognized by its thick, leathery leaves with striate venation. Somewhat similar to *Aerides* (see page 68), the flowers are borne in dense, pendent inflorescences. They are rather large, with a backward-pointing, flattened spur.

The plants require warm, humid, shady conditions for good growth. They grow well in hanging baskets so that their aerial roots hang freely. Warm.

R. gigantea A species from Burma and Thailand with long, thick leaves. The waxy flowers are varied in colour, white, pink or reddish purple, and up to 2.5 cm (1 in) across. Winter.

R. retusa A species from Java that usually has longer stems but smaller flowers. They are usually white, spotted with rose-pink and a pink lip. Summer.

R. violacea A widespread species in southeast Asia. The waxy flowers have white sepals, spotted petals and a dark mauve lip. Winter.

ROSSIOGLOSSUM

The six species of this genus are sometimes known as the clown orchids because of the shape of the callus at the base of the lip. They are distributed in Central America between Mexico and Panama. All the plants have dull, bluish green leaves and pseudobulbs. The inflorescences arise from the base of the plants, and each bears four to twenty large flowers, which are bright yellow, heavily barred or marked with chestnut brown.

Plants grow well in a shallow pot or basket with freely draining compost, or mounted on a slab of bark. They start their new growth in late spring and should be watered well and fertilized during the summer and until after flowering in the autumn or early winter. Then the plants need drier and cooler conditions until they start to grow again in spring.

R. grande This species comes from Guatemala and has the largest flowers in the genus, but only three to five of them. Autumn.

R. insleayi This species is limited to Mexico. It has smaller flowers but more of them than *R. grande*, up to 20 in a raceme. Winter.

R. schlieperianum This is a Costa Rican species that has medium sized flowers marked with greenish yellow instead of brown. Autumn.

SOBRALIA

A small genus of very showy terrestrial orchids from tropical America. The stems are tall and reed-like, sometimes up to 3 m (10 ft) tall, with alternate, plicate leaves. The large flowers last only a few days, but they appear in succession from the apex of the stem over a long period during midsummer.

The plants take up a lot of space in a small greenhouse, but they are easy subjects to look after in a conservatory or planted out in a tropical garden. They have the advantage of being evergreen and of having architectural interest even when not in flower. Provided with a large pot of freely draining compost and plenty of moisture, they will accept a wide range of environmental conditions.

S. macrantha The best-known species is actually a swamp grower in Mexico and Costa Rica and is 90–200 cm (3–6 ft) tall. The huge flowers vary from 15 to 25 cm (6 to 10 in) across, and are brilliant rose-pink with a magenta lip. A white form is also known. Summer.

S. xantholeuca A beautiful yellow-flowered species from Guatemala, of similar size and dimensions to *S. macrantha* but of different flower structure. Summer.

× SOPHROCATTLEYA (Sc.), × SOPHROLAELIA (Sl.) and × SOPHROLAELIOCATTLEYA (Slc.)

The so-called red cattleyas are intergeneric hybrids with one of the *Sophronitis* species, usually *S. coccinea*, in their ancestry as well as *Cattleya* or *Laelia* or both.

They are usually smaller plants than

other *Cattleya* hybrids, and easier to grow in cooler conditions. To produce the most intense colours in the flowers, the plants should be moved to a warm, bright place as they come into bud. Some of the smaller plants have become very popular because they take up so little space in the greenhouse. Recommended hybrids are × *Sc.* Batemaniana; × *Sl.* Psyche and Jinn; × *Slc.* Jewel Box 'Scheherezade' and 'Dark Waters', Falcon 'Westonbirt', Madge Fordyce and Hazel Boyd.

SOPHRONITIS

There are about ten species of the dwarf *Sophronitis*, confined to the mountains of Brazil and Paraguay. They are all epiphytic or lithophytic plants, with clusters of dark green or purplish pseudobulbs each with a single leaf and bright pink, red or orange flowers.

The plants grow best when mounted on slabs of bark or in small pots, but are sometimes hard to establish. They need shady, moist conditions with cool temperatures but a buoyant atmosphere.

S. cernua Flowers in clusters of up to ten, bright cinnabar red. Autumn.

S. coccinea (*S. grandiflora*) Flowers usually single, bright orange-red with a yellow

× *Potinara* Fortune Teller (see page 108)

Rhynchostylis gigantea from Thailand (see page 109)

Sophronitis coccinea
from Brazil

base to the lip in the typical form. A number of distinct colour variants have been described, including var. *barboleta*, peach-coloured; var. *pallens*, orange; var. *purpurea*, purple; and var. *rossiteriana*, yellow. Winter.

S. wittigiana The flowers are usually large and solitary, rose-pink. Winter.

STANHOPEA

A small genus of tropical orchids in the Americas that have exciting flowers of complex structure and are very strongly scented. They are large flowers and always on pendulous inflorescences. The swollen buds develop quickly during the summer months, and their opening is eagerly and attentively awaited. Unfortunately the exotic flowers last only a few days, never more than a week, and are produced only once a year.

Nevertheless, for the rest of the year the plants are very little trouble. They need to be accommodated in hanging baskets, from which the inflorescence at the base of the pseudobulbs can easily escape. The baskets can be hung from the roof of a humid greenhouse. The plants must be watered frequently during the growing season. Intermediate.

S. oculata A Central American species with five to eight flowers in each inflorescence. They are pale creamy yellow and covered with spots in the form of dull red circles. Summer.

S. tigrina A Mexican species with two to four showy flowers, which are a vivid golden orange, blotched with maroon. Summer.

Stanhopea wardii
from Peru (see
page 112)

S. wardii (*S. aurea*, *S. venusta*) A wide-spread species from Central America to Peru. The inflorescence bears eight to ten flowers, which are creamy yellow with small purplish dots. Summer.

STENOGLOTTIS

Six species of lithophytic orchids in this genus occur in Africa from Tanzania south to the eastern Cape. They are easy in cultivation and two are commonly grown in shallow pots, with a small amount of a peat-based compost over plenty of drainage material. They produce a rosette of leaves in early spring, which develop during the summer months. A raceme of many lilac flowers arises from the centre of the plant in later summer or autumn. Cool, intermediate or on a windowsill.

S. fimbriata This species comes from fairly cool habitats. The leaves have an undulate margin and are heavily marked with purplish spots. The small lilac flowers have a three-lobed lip.

S. longifolia A warmer-growing species than *S. fimbriata*, with plain green or lightly spotted leaves. The tall inflorescences bear many flowers with a five-lobed lip, and are long-lasting.

VANDA

The vandas give their name to the distinctive habit of growth, vandaceous, that they share with a large number of tropical orchids from the Old World. About 40 species are distributed in tropical Asia, from India east to Taiwan and southeast to Australia and the Solomon Islands. They all have a stout, upright stem bearing two rows of leathery leaves and many aerial roots. Inflorescences of very showy flowers arise in the leaf axils towards the top of the stem.

Plants grow well in large pots or hanging baskets in a bark-based compost. They require bright light, high humidity and, for many, a considerable amount of warmth.

V. coerulea This is one of the species from India; it needs a cooler, drier period during the winter months, after flowering. A winter minimum of 5–10°C (40–50°F) suits it well. The flowers are large, in a wide range of shades of bluish violet, pale or dark, and some pinkish colours. Summer.

V. coerulescens A smaller species than *V. coerulea*, from Burma and Thailand, but the flowers are the same lovely bluish violet, with a darker lip. Spring.

V. tricolor (*V. suavis*)–A robust species from Java and Laos. The flowers are white or light yellow, densely spotted with reddish brown, and the lip bright magenta purple. Various.

Hybrids Many beautiful hybrids are grown, particularly in the tropics. The most famous is the violet-blue *V. Rothschildiana* (*V. coerulea* × *Euanthe sanderiana*). *Euanthe* (see page 91), which is often included in the genus *Vanda*, is in the background of many of the hybrids, and passes on its round, flat shape and large size to its progeny. Recommended hybrids are Nellie Morley, Josephine van Brero and Deva (pink shades); Rothschildiana, Fuchs' Delight, Onomea and Hilo Blue (blue shades).

Vanda species and hybrids have also been crossed with other genera to produce some very striking intergeneric hybrids. The most commonly cultivated of these is × *Ascocenda*, crossed with *Ascocentrum* (see pages 70 and 71).

VANILLA

Few people realize that the flavouring called vanilla comes from the fruit of an orchid – and a most unusual one. There are about 100 different species of *Vanilla* in the tropical parts of the world. They are all vines, with long, scrambling stems bearing a broad leaf and a root at each node. A few are leafless. The inflorescences are borne on side shoots and bear a number of short-lived flowers in succession.

The vines can be started from a short cutting inserted in a peat-based compost, and can be trained along the walls and inside the roof of a greenhouse or conservatory. They need warm, shady, humid conditions to grow well, and tend to flower only when they have attained a considerable length and reach the brightest light near the glass. Intermediate to warm.

V. imperialis A very striking species from tropical Africa with robust stems and large leaves. The flowers are lime green with a large purple-streaked lip. Summer.

V. planifolia (*V. fragrans*) A tropical American species that is widely cultivated in Mexico, Réunion and Tahiti for its fruits, which are set after the flowers are Ipollinated by hand. Its flowers are yellowish green. Summer.

× VUYLSTEKEARA (Vuyl.)

One of the earliest of the hybridizers in the *Odontoglossum* alliance was C. Vuylsteke of Belgium, and this group of trigeneric hybrids was named in his honour. All the plants have the genera *Odontoglossum*, *Cochlioda* and *Miltonia* in their ancestry. Many result from crosses between odontiodas and miltonias.

They grow well in intermediate night temperatures combined with high humidity and plenty of fresh air. They are mostly coloured in shades of pink or red, with a large lip derived from the *Miltonia* parentage. Recommended hybrids are Cambria 'Plush' and 'Lensing's Favourite', Edna 'Stamperland' and Essendon.

× WILSONARA (Wils.)

This is one of the earliest trigeneric hybrids, in which representatives of three different genera, *Cochlioda*, *Odontoglossum* and *Oncidium*, have contributed to new orchids. In effect, they are usually crosses between x *Odontioda* and *Oncidium* or x *Odontocidium*. Many of these hybrids have been made with very colourful *Odontioda* crosses, and the resulting progeny also have bright colours, often on long and branching inflorescences. Recommended hybrids are Widecombe Fair, Anaway, Tigerwood, Celle, Autumn Leaves, Comitan and Kendrick Wiliams.

ZYGOPETALUM

There are about 40 species of *Zygopetalum* growing as epiphytes or terrestrials in the montane forests of tropical South America. In cultivation they grow well with cymbidiums, and also resemble them in growth habit, with a cluster of leaf-bearing pseudobulbs growing upright from a creeping rhizome. The inflorescences are erect with one or several showy flowers, which are remarkable for the bluish or violet colours in the lip. The plants have thick, succulent roots, so need large pots to accommodate them and a freely draining compost. Cool.

Z. B.G. White This is one of the most intensely coloured of a small range of hybrids that have been raised; the lip is deep violet. Autumn and winter.

Z. intermedium This is the finest species. The flowers are large, the sepals and petals are greenish but heavily spotted with dark brown purple, and the lip is white, striped with violet and softly hairy. The hyacinth-like fragrance on a sunny morning in winter is a delightful feature. Autumn and winter.

Orchids for Selected Situations

ORCHIDS FOR A WINDOWSILL

Brassavola nodosa
Cattleya aurantiaca
C. bowringiana
C. intermedia
Coelogyne cristata
C. flaccida
C. nitida
Cymbidium devonianum
C. eburneum
C. floribundum
Cymbidium Minuet
Cymbidium Peter Pan
Cymbidium Showgirl
Cymbidium Touchstone

Dendrobium kingianum
D. nobile
Encyclia aromatica
E. cochleata
E. cordigera
Laelia anceps
L. gouldiana
Lycaste aromatica
Maxillaria tenuifolia
Oncidium pulchellum
Paphiopedilum callosum
P. fairrieanum
P. insigne
Pleione species and hybrids

ORCHIDS FOR AN ENCLOSED CASE IN THE LIVING ROOM

Brassia maculata
B. verrucosa
Cattleya Bow Bells
   and other hybrids
Dendrobium bigibbum
Encyclia fragrans
Ludisia discolor
Paphiopedilum barbatum

P. callosum
Paphiopedilum Maudiae
P. sukhakulii
Phalaenopsis amabilis
P. lueddemanniana
P. schilleriana
Phalaenopsis hybrids

ORCHIDS FOR GROWING INDOORS UNDER LIGHTS

Ada aurantiaca
Aerides roseum
Brassia verrucosa
Cattleya Bow Bells and
   small-growing hybrids
Dendrobium bigibbum

Dendrochilum glumaceum
Paphiopedilum species and hybrids
Phalaenopsis species and hybrids
Rhynchostylis gigantea
Zygopetalum intermedium

ORCHIDS FOR THE GARDEN

Cymbidium goeringii
Cypripedium acaule
C. calceolus
C. debile
C. reginae

Dactylorhiza species and hybrids
Epipactis gigantea
E. palustris
Orchis morio

ORCHIDS FOR THE ALPINE HOUSE OR UNHEATED CONSERVATORY

Bletilla striata
Calanthe discolor
C. striata
Cymbidium goeringii

Cypripedium species
Habenaria radiata
Pleione species and hybrids

ORCHIDS FOR THE COOL HOUSE
Minimum night temperature 10°C (50°F)

Ada aurantiaca
Cochlioda species
Coelogyne cristata
Cuitlauzina pendula
Cymbidium species and hybrids
Dendrobium aphyllum
D. chrysotoxum
D. densiflorum
D. kingianum
D. moniliforme
D. nobile and its hybrids
D. speciosum
D. thyrsiflorum
Dracula species
Dryadella species
Masdevallia species and hybrids
Disa uniflora and hybrids
Lemboglossum bictoniense
L. cervantesii
L. maculatum
L. rossii

Lycaste species and hybrids
Odontoglossum crispum
Odontoglossum species and hybrids
× Odontioda hybrids
Oncidium incurvum
O. ornithorhynchum
Osmoglossum pulchellum
Paphiopedilum insigne
P. spicerianum
P. villosum
Pleione species and hybrids
Pleurothallis species
Rossioglossum grande
Sophronitis cernua
S. coccinea
Stenoglottis fimbriata
S. longifolia
Vanda coerulea
× Vuylstekeara hybrids
× Wilsonara hybrids

ORCHIDS FOR THE INTERMEDIATE HOUSE
Minimum night temperature 13°C (55°F)

Angraecum eburneum
A. leonis
A. sesquipedale
Angraecum Veitchii
Ansellia africana
Brassavola nodosa
Brassia species
× *Brassocattleya* hybrids
× *Brassolaeliocattleya* hybrids
Cattleya species and hybrids
Coelogyne dayana
C. speciosa
Dendrochilum glumaceum

Encyclia fragrans
Habenaria rhodocheila
× *Laeliocattleya* hybrids
Miltoniopsis species and hybrids
Oncidium species and hybrids
Paphiopedilum species and hybrids
Phragmipedium species and hybrids
× *Potinara* hybrids
Sobralia macrantha
× *Sophrolaeliocattleya* hybrids
Stanhopea species
Vanilla species

ORCHIDS FOR THE WARM HOUSE
Minimum night temperature 16–18°C (60–65°F)

Aerides species
Ascocentrum species
× *Ascocenda* hybrids
Calanthe triplicata
× *Doritaenopsis* hybrids
Doritis pulcherrima
Euanthe sanderiana
Ludisia discolor

Oncidium lanceanum
O. pulchellum
O. splendidum
Phalaenopsis species and hybrids
Renanthera species
Rhynchostylis species
Vanda species and hybrids

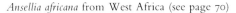

Ansellia africana from West Africa (see page 70)

Glossary

acuminate Gradually tapering to a long slender point or acumen.

apical At the tip.

axil The angle between the upper side of a leaf, branch or bract and the stem, or axis, from which it grows.

axillary Growing in an axil.

backbulb Old pseudobulb at the back of the plant, away from the growing point, and usually without leaves.

basal Leaves that arise from the base of the plant, not carried on the stem.

botrytis A fungus which appears as many small black or brown dots.

bract A small leaf, or leaf-like structure, in the axil of which a flower is borne.

calcareous Chalky or limestone.

callus (calli) A solid protuberance or growth caused by a mass of cells.

capsule A dry fruit that splits open at maturity to release its seeds.

clonal Derived from a single individual by the growth of buds or divisions.

clone An individual plant.

column The central part of the orchid flower, formed by the union of the stamen, style and stigma.

corm An enlarged, fleshy stem base.

crest A ridge, usually on the lip, often decorated or fringed.

crispate Having an irregular, curly margin.

cultivar A variant of any species or hybrid that is considered distinct from the horticultural point of view.

dormant Parts of the plant that are not in active growth.

embryo The rudimentary plant, still enclosed in the seed.

epiphyte (epiphytic) A plant that grows on other plants but not as a parasite.

equitant Folded lengthwise so that the base of each leaf enfolds the next.

genus (genera) The smallest natural group of plants containing distinct species.

generic Relating to a genus or genera.

glaucous Leaves that are covered with a greyish, waxy coat, as with cabbage leaves, bluish green.

grex A group, applied collectively to the progeny of any cross between two plants.

hermaphrodite Flowers that contain both the male and female reproductive organs.

hybrid A cross between two plants, usually of different species or even different genera, but it may also be between different forms, varieties or cultivars.

hypha (hyphae) Cylindrical, thread-like branches of the body of a fungus.

inflorescence The arrangement of flowers on the flowering stem.

intergeneric Between or among two or more genera.

keel A median, lengthwise ridge.

keiki A small plant arising from the stem or pseudobulb of a mature plant.

labellum The lip, or lowermost petal, of an orchid flower; usually held on the lower side of the flower and different in form from the other two petals.

lateral sepals The pair of similar sepals arranged at the sides of an orchid flower.

lax Loose or distant, as opposed to tightly or densely arranged.

lip The labellum, or odd petal of an orchid flower; usually held on the lower side of the flower and different in shape, colour and size from the other two petals.

lithophyte A plant that lives on a rock.

mentum A chin-like projection formed at the base of the lip or by the united bases of the lateral sepals.

meristem A group of unspecialized cells capable of division and becoming specialized to form new tissues of the plant.

monopodial A stem with a single, continuous axis.

multigeneric Involving more than two genera in the parentage.

mycorrhiza The symbiotic union of a fungus with the roots of a plant.

node A point on a stem where a leaf is attached.

nomenclatural Relating to names.

ovary The part of the flower that contains the ovules; an immature fruit.

ovate Egg-shaped in outline, usually pointed at the apex, wider towards the base.

ovoid Egg-shaped.

panicle A branching inflorescence in which all the branches bear flowers.

papilla (papillae) Small, fleshy protuberance on the surface of the leaf or flower.

papillose A surface that is covered with papillae.

peaty Resembling peat, the soil that is found in bogs and on some moors and is fibrous and acid.

pedicel The term used for the stalk of a flower.

peduncle The stalk of an inflorescence.

pendent, pendulous Hanging downwards or inclined.

perennial A plant that lasts for several years.

petiole The stalk of a leaf.

petiolate Having a petiole.

plicate Folded like a fan; pleated.

pollinium (pollinia) A body composed of many pollen grains cohering together.

pollinarium The structure that is carried from one flower to another to achieve pollination, usually consisting of one or more pollinia which are attached to the viscidium by a caudicle or stalk.

propagule An offset or other small division from which new plants will grow.

protocorm A round or tuber-like structure that is the first stage of growth from the embryo to the adult plant.

pseudobulb The thickened stem or stem base of many orchid plants, but not a true bulb.

raceme An unbranched inflorescence in which the flowers are borne on short pedicels and usually open in succession from the base upwards.

rachis The flower-bearing portion of an inflorescence.

rhizoid A small outgrowth like a root hair.

rhizome A root-like stem that creeps under or over the ground or other surface, sending roots downwards and branches, leaves or flowering shoots upwards. It is always distinguished from a root by the presence of leaves or scales and buds.

sepals The three outermost parts of the flower.

sessile Without a stalk.

sheath The lower portion of the leaf, clasping the stem; also used for bracts that enclose the flowering stem below those that support the flowers.

species A group of individuals that exhibit the same distinctive characteristics; the unit that provides the basis for classification.

spike An unbranched inflorescence bearing sessile flowers; in orchids sometimes used as a general term for flowering stems with many flowers.

staminode A sterile stamen; a structure appearing in the place of a stamen but bearing no pollen.

stigma, stigmatic surface The sticky area on the column that receives the pollen or pollinarium in pollination.

stomata Breathing pores or apertures in the surface of plants.

symbiosis The living together of dissimilar organisms with benefit to one or both.

symbiotic Relating to symbiosis.

tessellated With paler or darker markings that have rather square edges, as in Roman mosaic pavements.

trigeneric Involving three genera in the parentage.

terete Cylindrical, like a pencil; circular in cross-section.

terrestrial On or in the ground.

tuber A thickened branch of an underground stem that produces buds; like a potato. Also, a swollen root or branch of a root that serves as a store of reserve food; like a dahlia.

umbel, umbellate An inflorescence in which the diverging pedicels, all of the same length, arise from the same point at the apex of the peduncle.

undulate With a wavy margin or surface.

vandaceous With a habit of growth similar to that of the genus *Vanda*, *i.e.* monopodial, with the leaves in two rows.

variety (var.) A subdivision of a species that is easily recognized by its different size, colour or other minor modification; in gardening circles often loosely used instead of cultivar.

velamen The absorbent covering of the roots of many orchids.

viscidium (viscidia) The sticky gland by which the pollinarium is carried from one flower to another.

Bibliography

GENERAL WORKS ON ORCHIDS AND THEIR CULTIVATION

Bechtel, H., Cribb, P.J. and Launert, E. *Manual of Cultivated Orchid Species* (Blandford Press, 3rd edition, 1992)

Bristow, A. *Orchids* (Cassell/Royal Horticultural Society, 1985)

Dunmire, J.R. *Orchids* (Sunset, 1999)

Elliott, J. (editor). *Orchid Growing in the Tropics* (OSSEA (Singapore) Times Editions, 1993)

Fast, G. *Orchideenkultur* (Ulmer, 1995)

Noble, M. *You Can Grow Orchids* (Mary Noble McQuerry, 5th edition, 1987)

Northen, R.T. *Home Orchid Growing* (Prentice Hall Press, 4th edition, 1990)

Northen, R.T. *Miniature Orchids* (Van Nostrand Reinhold, 1980)

Pridgeon, A. *The Illustrated Encyclopoedia of Orchids* (Headline, 1992)

Rittershausen, B. and W. *Orchid Growing Illustrated* (Blandford Press, 1985)

Stewart, J. and Griffiths, M. *The RHS Manual of Orchids* (Macmillan, 1995)

Watson, J. (ed.) *Growing Orchids* (American Orchid Society, 1998)

Williams, B. (ed.) *Orchids for Everyone* (Hamlyn, 1987)

WORKS ON INDIVIDUAL GENERA

Chase, M.W. (ed.) *The Pictorial Encyclopoedia of Oncidium* (1997)

Cribb, P.J. and Butterfield, I. *The Genus Pleione* (Natural History Publications (Borneo), 2nd edition, 1999)

Cribb, P.J. *The Genus Paphiopedilum* Second Edition (Natural History Publications (Borneo), 1998)

Du Puy, D.J. and Cribb, P.J. *The Genus Cymbidium* (Christopher Helm, 1988)

Grove, D.L. *Vandas and Ascocendas* (Timber Press, 1995)

Halbinger, F. and Soto, M. *Laelias of Mexico* (1997)

Motes, M.R. *Vandas* (Timber Press, 1997)

Schelpe, S. and Stewart, J. *Dendrobiums, an introduction to the species in cultivation* (Orchid Sundries Ltd., 1990)

Withner, C.L. *The Cattleyas and their Relatives* (Timber Press, six volumes, 1988–2000)

BOOKS ON WILD ORCHIDS IN VARIOUS PARTS OF THE WORLD

Africa

la Croix, I.F., la Croix, E.A.S. and la Croix T.M. *Orchids of Malawi* (A.A. Balkema, 1991)

la Croix, I.F. and la Croix, E. *African Orchids in the Wild and in Cultivation* (Timber Press, 1997)

Linder, H.P. and Kurzweil, H. *Orchids of Southern Africa* (Balkema, 1999)

Stewart, J. and Campbell, B. *Orchids of Kenya* (St. Paul's Bibliographies, 1996)

Wodrich, K. *Growing South African Indigenous Orchids* (A.A. Balkema, 1997)

America

Dressler, R.L. *Field Guide to the Orchids of Costa Rica and Panama* (Cornell, 1993)

Escobar, Rodrigo, R. *Native Colombian Orchids* (Editorial Collina, Medellin, 6 volumes, 1990-1994)

Keenan, P.E. *Wild Orchids across North America* (Timber Press, 1998)

Luer, C. *The Native Orchids of Florida* (New York Botanic Garden, 1972)

Luer, C. *The Native Orchids of the United States and Canada* (New York Botanic Garden, 1975)

Miranda, F. *Orchids from the Brazilian Amazon* (Editora Expressao e cultura, 1996)

Asia

Comber, J.B. *Orchids of Java* (Bentham Moxon Trust, Kew, 1990)

Kamemoto, H. and Sagarik, R. *Beautiful Thai Orchid Species* (The Orchid Society of Thailand, 1975)

Seidenfaden, G.L. and Wood, J.J. *The Orchids of Peninsular Malaysia and Singapore* (Olsen and Olsen, Denmark, 1992)

Australia

Hoffman, N. and Brown, A. *Orchids of South-West Australia* (University of Western Australia Press, 2nd edition, 1992)

Jones, D.L. *Orchids of Australia* (Reed, 1988)

Lavarack, P.S. and Gray, B. *Tropical Orchids of Australia* (Nelson, 1985)

Europe

Bournerias, M. *Les Orchidees de France, Belgique et Luxembourg* (Parthenope Collection, Paris, 1998)

Buttler, K.P. *Field Guide to the Orchids of Britain and Europe* (The Crowood Press, 1991)

Cribb, P.J. and Bailes, C. *Hardy Orchids* (Timber Press, 1989)

Delforge, P. *Orchids of Britain and Europe* (Harper Collins, 1995)

Curtis's *Botanical Magazine*. This publication still maintains its long tradition of fine colour printing and articles on plants, plant collecting and conservation. Since it was established in 1787 nearly 10,500 colour plates, including about 1200 orchids to date, have appeared by many of the best British botanical artists.

Acknowledgements

I warmly thank my former colleagues Sandra Bell and Phillip Cribb for reading the manuscript, and for their comments and Ron Hayward for the line drawings.

Photographs
Bob Campbell, pages 66–7, 78, 79 (top), 82 (bottom), 87, 90 (bottom), 99 (top and bottom), 111 (bottom); Carmen Coll, pages 30, 79 (bottom), 86 (top and bottom), 110 (bottom); Eric Crichton Photos, pages 22, 23, 34, 38, 42, 43, 46, 47, 50, 54, 70 (top and bottom), 74, 98 (bottom), 103 (bottom); Crown copyright © reproduced with the permission of the Controller, Her Majesty's Stationery Office, and the Director, Royal Botanic Gardens, Kew, pages 6, 10, 19; Bruce Eden, page 71; Stephen G. Haw, page 63; Brian Mathew, pages 83 (bottom), 106 (bottom); Bill Pottinger, pages 94, 103 (top); Joyce Stewart, pages 26, 51, 55, 58, 62, 75 (top and bottom), 82 (top), 83 (top), 90 (top), 91, 95, 98 (top), 102, 106 (top), 107, 110 (top), 111 (top); Zefa Picture Library, page 14.

Index

Page numbers in italics indicate illustrations d = line drawing